D1443184

MODES OF OCCURRENCE

Barry Taylor

Modes of Occurrence

Verbs, Adverbs and Events

Aristotelian Society Series

Volume 2

Basil Blackwell · Oxford

© Barry Taylor 1985

First published 1985
in cooperation with The Aristotelian Society
King's College, London WC2R 2LS

Basil Blackwell Publisher Ltd
108 Cowley Road, Oxford OX4 1JF, England

Basil Blackwell Inc.
432 Park Avenue South, Suite 1505
New York, NY 10016, USA

British Library Cataloguing in Publication Data

Taylor, Barry
Modes of occurrence : verbs, adverbs
and events.
1. Languages—Philosophy   2. Grammar,
Comparative and general—Adverb
I. Title
149′.94   P106

ISBN 0–631–14026–3

Photoset and printed in Great Britain by
Photobooks (Bristol) Ltd

Contents

Preface

This book began as a doctoral thesis, submitted at Oxford just over ten years ago. Heartily sick of adverbs after writing that thesis, I contented myself with wrenching a couple of articles out of it, and turned with relief to other topics. Still, I felt that the earlier work retained some virtues; and, finding myself last year able once more to look an adverb in the face, I decided to revamp my old ideas for publication.

Not that this book simply reproduces my old thesis. For one thing, it is considerably shorter, and less cluttered with what I now perceive as irrelevant details. Further, some central tenets of my older views have been entirely reshaped: the eventual theory of adverbial structure advocated in my thesis was an ungainly thing, distorted by attempts to overcome a problem posed by Gareth Evans; I now think Evans' points can be met more neatly, and have been able to reformulate my semantics accordingly. Again, I now give very different arguments in favour of my general perspective on the theory of meaning. Finally, I have incorporated into this new version responses to criticisms which were drawn by previous publications.

I began this revamping of my views in an Aristotelian Society paper ('Events and Adverbs', *Proceedings of the Aristotelian Society* LXXIV (1983–4) pp. 103–122), in which I developed my new response to Evans' problem; and this book's discussion of that problem (in sections 2 and 3 of Chapter Five) is lifted from that paper. Further, I found it convenient simply

to take over from the same paper the current book's discussion
of the semantic problems adverbs raise (Chapter One, sections
4 to 8) and its rebuttal of some criticisms of my views (Chapter
Four, section 5 and part of section 6).

Other parts of this book also draw heavily on material I have
previously published. In particular, the theory of states of
affairs given in Chapter Two was first presented in a paper
'States of Affairs', published in 1976 by OUP in a collection of
essays called *Truth and Meaning* edited by Gareth Evans and
John McDowell (pp. 263–284). Many people seem to have
found that essay a hard read, and I have accordingly rewritten
it almost entirely in the hope of gaining greater perspicuity.
The theory presented, as the text notes, was inspired by a
construction of McKinsey's; I was surprised, after the initial
publication, also to see some of its main features anticipated in
a paper by van Fraassen (see Bibliography), though I find his
essay too tersely expressed to comprehend the connexions
fully. There are also obvious affinities between my views and
those subsequently expressed in writings by Barwise and Perry.

Again, my ideas on the continuous tense and the classification of verbs have been published previously, in a paper
called 'Tense and Continuity' in *Linguistics and Philosophy* 1
(1977) pp. 199–220[1], of which Chapter Three (save section 7) is
a virtual reprint. It transpires that, at the same time I was
developing these views in Oxford, Barbara Partee, Michael
Bennett and David Dowty were in America thinking along
broadly similar lines; and, by an odd quirk of fate, their work
finally surfaced into properly accessible publication in an
article by Dowty in the same volume of *Linguistics and
Philosophy* as my own. In a subsequent book (see Bibliography)
Dowty took me to task over the all-important details; I return
the compliment in this one.

I express my thanks to the editors and publishers of the
sources given for permission to make use of previously
published material. There are, in addition, many people I
should thank for helping me to clean up my ideas over the
years; in particular, I would like to list Christopher Arnold,
Roger Fellows, Lloyd Humberstone, Cynthia Macdonald,

Graham Macdonald, Christopher Peacocke, Mark Platts, Denis Robinson, Peter Strawson, and David Wiggins. Martin Davies has given me invaluable help working over this final version, which was patiently and ably typed by Josie Winther. I should also thank my University for six months study-leave to prepare this last draft, and the Philosophy Department at La Trobe University for proving to be such genial hosts whilst I was doing so. But my main debts are to John McDowell, who supervised part of the thesis from which this book springs and whose conversation has subtly shaped its final version; to Michael Dummett, who undertook the bulk of the supervisory role, and who taught me more about philosophy than the finished work will show; and to Gareth Evans, a source of tireless and powerful criticism and a good friend, to whose memory this book is dedicated.

A note finally about my syntactic conventions. My practice in this book has been to use expressions autonymously in more formal contexts, where a plethora of quotes is likely to overload the symbolism; in other contexts to use quotes, but not to bother with differentiating ordinary quotes from quasi-quotes (so that ordinary quotation is, where necessary, to be construed as quasi-quotation). To the purist who will justifiably complain at this lawless informality, my only response is that I have taken every care that it disguises no genuine use/mention confusion; and that I think it increases the book's readability, for everyone except enraged purists.

Barry Taylor
July, 1984

1

The Trouble with Adverbs

1.   When an Upsaroka addresses a sentence to his linguistic confrères, there is an ability they possess which is not shared by a monoglot European bystander: the ability to redescribe the utterance, antecedently characterizable merely as the issuance of such-and-such vocables, as an assertion that the wigwam is on fire, a demand that the squaws be liberated, a query whether every even number is the sum of two primes, . . . Generalizing, it appears then that what distinguishes *L*-speakers from the rest is the ability to redescribe an utterance of an *L*-sentence in a particular way – as an utterance performed in a specific *mode* (*i.e.* as a *speech-act* of a certain kind) and with a particular *content*. But we can be a little more precise than this.

I once saw a man in a pub raise his empty glass to his eye telescope-fashion and utter 'I see no ships'; his English-speaking audience unhesitatingly classified his utterance both as an assertion that he saw no ships, and as a request that his glass be refilled by whichever of his interlocutors whose turn it was to purchase the next round. But evidently this second classification is parasitic on the first. (It would never be sought at all if the first classification did not characterize the utterance as an assertion whose content is in the circumstances so bizarre; though at the same time, that bizarre content in some devious way conditions identification of the second classification's more mundane subject-matter – had my man uttered 'Sharks never sleep' in place of his 'I see no ships', most likely the second classification of his utterance would differ markedly in assignment of content, if indeed it was on at all.) Let us style a redescription of an utterance in terms of mode and content *primary* if not thus parasitic on another similar redescription. Then evidently the ability L-speakers essentially possess is characterizable more accurately as the ability to find *primary* redescriptions of utterances of L-sentences as being of a certain mode and with a particular content – for, our example suggests, a hearer slow on the uptake who failed with the secondary redescription would, though lacking in ability, not be lacking any specifically *linguistic* capacity.

The primary task of a theory of meaning for L is, plausibly, to articulate what it is that distinguishes L-speakers essentially from the rest; hence, to specify precisely the nature of the ability just described to find primary redescriptions of utterances of L-sentences. The bipartite nature of these redescriptions in turn suggests that such a theory will be naturally divided into two components: a *theory of force*, stating the conditions under which an utterance of an L-sentence is to be assigned a certain *mode*; and a *theory of sense*,[1] assigning *contents* to utterances whose mode the theory of force has fixed. The work of such speech-act theorists as Austin and Searle[2] gives us the broad shape of the theory of force for L: it will set out principles determining when an utterance counts as having a certain mode on the basis of the *intentions* of the utterer and/or features of the context of utterances rendered germane by *conventions* prevalent amongst L-speakers. But what should be the form of L's theory of sense?

The mode assigned to an utterance in a primary redescription potentially depends, as just noted, on a number of character-

---

[1] Here my terminology follows that of John McDowell, as developed *e.g.* in section 1 of his 'Truth Conditions'. Unfortunately, even amongst writers who make the same distinctions there is no standard terminology – *e.g.* Dummett in 'What is a Theory of Meaning? [II]' dubs my theory of sense the 'theory of reference', and means by the 'theory of sense' something quite different from what is intended here.

[2] See the former's *How to Do Things with Words* and the latter's *Speech Acts*.

istics of the utterance and its surroundings; but the sole relevant feature for determining content is apparently just the sentence uttered. (Recall that the redescription is to be primary; and abstract for the present from problems raised by indexicality.) Thus, an utterance of 'Die Tür ist offen' may, depending on context, be counted by German-speakers as an assertion, command, query, . . . ; but, in primary redescription, only as an assertion, command, query . . . concerning the door's being open. This suggests the theory of sense for L might take the simple form of a list, pairing each L-sentence with a content; but this simple model won't do, and not merely because L will normally contain infinitely many sentences, rendering the list incompletable. For it is a further fact about L-speakers that in assigning content to an utterance in primary redescription they proceed systematically, the assigned content depending in principled fashion on the particular primitive elements out of which the uttered sentence is constructed, and on the manner of the structuring. An adequate theory of meaning for L should seek to reflect this feature too of the L-speaker's distinctive ability; so its component theory of sense should aim beyond mere listwise pairing of sentences with contents, seeking rather a method of pairing which displays the relevance of structure.

One attractive model for a theory adequate to this task goes like this: L's theory of sense is an axiomatized theory, cast in a metalanguage ML for L, and incorporating a recursive syntax for the language. A subset of its axioms – its semantic axioms – display a recursive structure based upon that of the incorporated syntax: for each L-expression discerned by the syntax as primitive, there is a semantic axiom giving conditions under which appropriate semantic concepts come to apply to that expression; and, for each method of composition the syntax distinguishes, there is a further such axiom specifying the conditions under which semantic concepts apply to an expression formed by that method, in terms of concepts applicable to the expressions out of which it is generated. Finally, the theory contains a distinguished context $\mathscr{C}$ and a canonical proof-theory such that, for each indicative sentence S of L, there is a canonically-provable instance of the schema

[I] $\mathscr{C}\ (\bar{S},p)$

where $\bar{S}$ is a standard name in ML of S (*e.g.* a quotation-mark name of S, or a numeral for a Godel-number thereof), and 'p' is replaced by some used sentence of ML; and where the requirement of the canonical proof-theory is that, in proving such instances of [I], it invokes precisely those semantic axioms which concern syntactic primitives and compositional modes displayed in the S concerned, and invokes them moreover in an order determined by that in which the preferred syntax uses those modes to generate S from the given primitives. For indicative S, the canonical provability of an instance of [I] can then be identified with the theory's conventional way of asserting that, according to it,

the content associated with S is that p;

whilst, for nonindicative S, its content-assignment can be equated with that it assigns to S's indicative transform. And evidently in either case the requirements made of the canonical proof-theory, and the axiomatic structure it reflects, ensure that a theory of sense construed on this model will faithfully reflect the systematic dependence of content-assignment on syntactic structure.

Moreover, a simplification of the model presents itself. As described it allows each theory of sense to choose its own context $\mathscr{C}$ to specify its content-assignments, in the shape of instances of [I]. But, if the theory is to get its content-assignments right – if, that is, those assignments are to mesh properly with the theory of force to issue in primary redescriptions of utterances of L-sentences which genuinely match those made by L-speakers themselves – then evidently it should aim at generating only rather special instances of its version of [I]; namely those instances (as we might less blushingly have said in the days of pre-Quinean innocence) in which the sentence supplanting the schematic 'p' is the translation into ML of the L-sentence S with which the instance deals. This formulation suggests a link with Tarski's celebrated Convention T,[3] and the connexion can be made more precise:

---

[3] See 'The Concept of Truth', pp. 187–8.

if a theory of sense for L so chooses its $\mathscr{C}$ that its version of [I] has the form

[II] $\bar{S}$ is true-in-$L \leftrightarrow p$,

then it is construable also as a theory of truth for L, recursively assigning truth-conditions to each of L's indicative sentences; and (construed as a theory of sense) it gets its content-assignments right just in case (construed as a theory of truth) it is adequate by the lights of Convention T. There seems no reason why we should not generally require a theory of sense so to choose its $\mathscr{C}$ that its content assignments take the form of instances of [II] (*i.e.* of 'T-sentences', as such instances have come generally to be known), and the promise of fruitful integration with the Tarskian tradition if we do. Our model for the theory of sense for L thus becomes, in sum, that of a truth-theory for L meeting Tarski's Convention T.

The dialectical path just traversed will be familiar from the writings of Donald Davidson, and of those – such as John McDowell and others like Martin Davies – who have refined and elaborated his position; indeed, the whole point of the foregoing has been to set the framework of this essay firmly within the tradition these writers represent, and the interested reader is referred to their work for more subtle and detailed statement of the framework presupposed.[4] The conclusion reached, moreover – that the core of a theory of meaning for L should take the form of a theory of truth – may well seem more commonplace still, though this impression should be treated with some caution. For not everything the literature quite properly styles as being in some sense truth-theory will be the business of the theory of sense as I have characterized it. There is, for example, no justification extractable from the foregoing for the demand that a theory of sense cast in the form of a truth-theory should aim beyond the circumscription of truth-in-L *simpliciter* (via generation of appropriate T-sentences) to a more general delineation of truth-in-L relative to an arbitrary model, and indeed a truth-theory cast in the latter model-

---

[4] See *e.g.* Davidson's 'Truth and Meaning' and 'Semantics for Natural Languages'; McDowell's 'Truth-Conditions', and his 'On the Sense'; and Davies' *Meaning, Quantification, Necessity*.

theoretic form will typically as it stands achieve its generality by couching its assignments of truth-conditions in language charged with set-theory, hence in terms rendering those assignments less than suitable for construal as giving the content of the utterances *L*-speakers conceive themselves as making. (Of course, a characterization of truth-in-*L* *simpliciter* is often readily extractable from a model-theory, and with it a less extravagant phrasing of truth-condition assignments more apt for the ends of primary predescription – but then it is this extractable theory rather than the model-theory itself which is properly construed as *L*'s theory of sense.) Again, the perspective here adopted should lead us to view with some suspicion the claims to count as a theory of sense of a truth-theory which, in the style of Montague, makes heavy use of the apparatus of possible worlds. Suppose, for example, that a truth-theory, oversimplifying David Lewis's analysis,[5] generates the T-sentence

(1) 'If kangaroos were tailless, they would topple over' is true-in-English ↔ the world *w* which most resembles this one save that kangaroos in *w* are tailless in *w* is such that kangaroos in *w* topple over in *w*.

If we are prepared to allow the right-hand-side of (1) intelligible at all, we should also be prepared to allow that it assigns to the conditional with which it deals an appropriate truth-condition (*modulo* Lewisean niceties), and hence that it is apt to figure in a truth-theory for English adequate by *some* standard. What is more dubious is that that standard is Convention T (which is, after all, only a *sufficient* measure of a *truth-theory's* adequacy), since – even after all due allowance has been made for Quinean reservations about the concepts involved – it is unclear that the right-hand-side of (1) can by any criterion be counted a 'translation' of the conditional. And by the same token we should be hesitant to allow that a theory of truth containing (1) can be reckoned a theory of sense for English, since it is at least dubious that an *e.g.* assertive utterance of the conditional can properly be redescribed as an

[5] See his book *Counterfactuals*.

assertion that the right-hand-side of (1) obtains – as an assertion that the world w most resembling this one . . . (To maintain that that *was* an appropriate redescription would evidently be tendentiously to credit the standard English-speaker with grasp not just of such mundane concepts as *being a kangaroo*, but also of their world-relativized correlates, such as *being a kangaroo in w*, for variable w.) In sum, then, from the present perspective a theory of sense for L can take the form of a theory of truth; but only of a theory of truth conceived more austerely than, for other purposes, it need be.

2.   The principal problem this essay sets out to tackle is this: what are the complications engendered for the theory of sense of some language L, construed on the foregoing model as an appropriately-stated theory of truth for L, by the presence in L of adverbial constructions? – *i.e.*, for present rough purposes, of what we learn at school to classify as adverbs and prepositional phrases. But I simplify at once, by restricting primary attention just to English as one familiar language replete with adverbial constructions, in the expectation that any solution of the problem applicable to it will generalize easily enough. And I need a sharper formulation of my problem even in this primary, domestic application.

   According to the last section's model, a theory of sense for English (as for any language) incorporates a syntax, which displays each indicative sentence as constructed out of finitely many primitives through application of compositional modes drawn from a fixed list. We need not, however, suppose that the syntactic descriptions thus suited to the needs of the theory of sense will jejunely reflect the more evident or 'surface' contours of English sentences. For it is a familiar fact that words of English slide about amongst categories any naive grammar would have to regard as distinct (so that *e.g.* 'call' functions at this surface level as both noun and verb), prompting the suggestion that the way to semantic insight might be in imputing to English sentences a deeper structure, obscured by their surface shape, in which words march in a more disciplined fashion. And again, there is an appearance of excess about the plethora of grammatical constructions English manifests at the surface level, motivating a hunch that the theory of sense might face a simpler task if based on a syntax more meagre in its deployment of modes of composition. These considerations suggest that the syntax which founds a theory of sense for English should be bipartite in structure. First, it should recursively delineate a set of simple indicative sentences, the 'base sentences' of English according to the syntax: these will consist of pieces of English vocabulary restricted to what the syntax regards as their primary grammatical roles, held together by modes of composition the syntax construes as fundamental; they will be represented accordingly by the well-formed formulae of a symbolism with a vocabulary of regimented English, and designed for the perspicuous display of modes of composition. A second component of the syntax will consist of a set of specifications of syntactic operations or 'transformations' which, successively applied to base sentences, transmute them into surface sentences of everyday English with intuitively equivalent meaning – it being required of an adequate account that every sentence at the surface be thus obtainable from at least one sentence in the base, and that a surface sentence be derivable from two or more nonequivalent base elements just in case it is plausibly construed as structurally ambiguous, with one base paraphrase corresponding to each of its meanings. Assuming this structure in the syntax on which it is based, it follows that the theory of sense need busy itself directly only with the base sentences its grammar discerns, its content-assignments to surface sentences being identifiable with the assignments it makes to the base paraphrases from which those sentences transformationally derive.

(All this talk of surface sentences deriving from a 'base' by a series of meaning-preserving 'transformations' is strongly redolent of Chomsky's *Aspects* model for English grammar, whose familiar terminology I have found it natural to adopt. But notice that this apparatus is used here only in the limited context of issuing syntactic descriptions amenable to the requirements of the theory of sense, not for the global Chomskyan enterprise of the generative delineation of the set of grammatical English sentences. Sentences apt to form a base

suited to the present local ends need not accordingly be suited
to the role of base for an *Aspects* grammar, nor vice versa
(indeed, there is no particular reason why the base sentences
the syntax of the theory of sense discerns should exist on *any*
generative level of *Aspects* grammar, except where they chance
to correspond to literal surface English); and again, transformations are not asked in the present context to bear the
explanatory weight of those in the *Aspects* framework, and
labour accordingly under fewer constraints. It follows further
that nothing said above about the structure of the syntax
presupposed by the theory of sense commits us to the primacy
of the *Aspects* model for global syntax – and a good thing too,
given the revisions of and rivals to that model proposed by a
host of later writers, not least Chomsky himself. At the same
time, it would of course be nice if the syntax of the theory of
sense were *somehow* neatly to mesh with an eventual global
syntax, construed according to whatever pattern the linguists
find eventually to predominate. What makes it difficult to say
anything more definite than this is the current state of total if
fruitful controversy amongst linguists as to what that pattern
might be, compounded by a further complication – that the
debate amongst them turns at points upon semantic considerations not always legitimate from the standpoint of the
present essay, with its requirement that issues of meaning be
elucidated via the theory of sense.)

Assuming the syntax of the theory of sense for English to
take the bipartite transformational shape just sketched, then,
and casting that theory in the form of a truth-theory, our
concern with the theory of sense for English becomes that of
constructing an adequate theory of truth, austerely conceived,
for a symbolism apt to express the language's base sentences.
Now we learn in elementary logic classes how to render a host
of surface English sentences into first-order notation, *i.e.* into a
symbolism where English vocabulary is regimented into the
categories of n-place predicates and functors, and well-formed
formulae are built up by constructions of predication,
functional application, truth-functional composition, and
quantification of individual variables. And Tarski taught us a
general method whereby, given any such first-order L, an
austerely adequate truth-theory for L might be constructed in a

metalanguage *ML* which is similarly first-order, provided only
that we know how *L*'s primitive vocabulary translates into *ML*;
further, the natural way of deriving T-sentences in such a
Tarskian truth-theory has the structure the last section
demanded of the canonical proof-theory in a theory of sense.[6]
Suppose then we choose to construe the familiar first-order
paraphrases of surface English sentences as the base paraphrases those sentences receive in the syntax of the theory of
sense. (The only bar to such a construal would be the
impossibility of articulating suitable transformations linking
these base paraphrases with their surface equivalents; and,
while no attempt will be made here to carry out the fiddly task
of actually providing such an articulation, the presumption
must surely be that a modicum of ingenuity would be enough
to achieve it, the more so given the permissiveness with which
we can view transformations in the present context.) And
suppose further we decide – why not? – to write the sense-giving
theory of truth we seek in first-order language using the same
regimented English vocabulary as the base sentences themselves deploy, so that primitive elements of the base trans-
late homophonically into the language of the theory. Then
Tarski's method straightforwardly applied will construct all
that part of the truth-theory we seek which deals with the host
of surface English sentences amenable to first-order paraphrase.

   The primary difficulties in constructing a theory of truth for
English apt to function as a theory of sense come thus to centre
around those devices whose presence in the language is
responsible for the existence of surface sentences which resist
first-order paraphrase. Foremost among these are indexical
devices, to accommodate sentences containing which we need
apparently to propose base structures which extend first-order

---

[6] For details of Tarski's method, see 'The Concept of Truth'; especially
section 3. By 'the natural way' for deriving T-sentences in a Tarskian theory, I
mean of course that exemplified in Tarski's own derivation of a sample T-
sentence on p. 196 of his classic paper. It is a simple enough formal exercise to
describe the procedures deployed in such natural derivations in terms
sufficiently general to construct the required notion of a canonical proof; the
description will be similar to that given by Davies (*Meaning*, p. 33) for his Tθ,
but generalized to take account of satisfaction as well as truth.

resources, and a corresponding extension to Tarskian methods to construct a theory of truth capable of embracing them – but I have given my views on these complications elsewhere,[7] and shall accordingly in the present work for the most part abstract from the complexities they engender. But also to be counted troublesome are those adverbial constructions which are my immediate present concern, and my problem with them can now be stated in the sharper terms I sought back at the beginning of this section: to what extent, if any, do English adverbial constructions force us to complicate the base structures of English beyond the merely first-order? And what complications, if any, must correspondingly be made to Tarskian methods to yield a theory of truth embracing adverbial constructions and apt to serve as a theory of sense?

3. Consider some straightforward sentence like

(2) Brutus stabbed Caesar

and then some sentences which arise from adorning it with adverbial structure, such as

(3) Brutus stabbed Caesar violently
(4) Brutus stabbed Caesar with a knife
(5) Brutus stabbed Ceasar violently with a knife
(6) Brutus stabbed Caesar with a knife violently.

Evidently, straightforward (2) – abstracting, in line with policy, from the indexical feature of its tense – is renderable at once in purely first-order terms as

(2i) Stab(Brutus,Caesar).

So the problems adverbial constructions pose for first-order base structures ought to emerge as those which arise in attempting to find similar renderings for (3)–(6).

Yet at first glance it might seem no such problems arise. For when learning logic we are taught how to give first-order paraphrases of (3)–(6), rendering them as

[7] See my 'Truth Theory'.

(3i) Stab-violently(Brutus,Caesar)
(4i) $(\exists x)(\text{Knife}(x)$ & Stab-with(Brutus,Caesar,x))
(5i) $(\exists x)(\text{Knife}(x)$ &
      Stab-violently-with(Brutus,Caesar,x))
(6i) $(\exists x)(\text{Knife}(x)$ &
      Stab-with-violently(Brutus,Caesar,x)).

But in construing these renditions, we must be careful to recall that they treat the constituent predicates of stabbing – the two-place 'Stab-violently' and 'Stab-with', and the three-place 'Stab-violently-with' and 'Stab-with-violently' – as logical primitives independent of each other as of the simple 'Stab' of (2i), any appearance they may have of sharing common elements being an artefact merely of the notation here chosen to represent them. And reflection on the consequences of this logical independence is enough to discredit these learners'-logic paraphrases as genuinely adequate.

To start with, there is the fact that they fail to reflect the complex logical connexions which hold between the un-analysed (2)–(6). Thus (3) and (4) both entail (2) by an inference pattern we may dub 'adverbial elimination', which is further exemplified in the entailment of (3) by (5) and of (4) by (6). Again, (5) and (6) co-entail each other by a procedure we may term 'adverbial commutation'. And further entailments amongst our sample sentences arise by iteration and combination of these processes. Yet none of these entailments is mirrored by logical relations between the purported paraphrases (2i)–(6i).

It is perhaps sufficient reply to this initial objection, thus baldly stated, that the entailments between (2)–(6), though not by the lights of (2i)–(6i) purely logical, can be articulated as entailments nevertheless, by laying down mediating *non*logical axioms or 'meaning postulates' linking the logically independent predicates of the paraphrases. Still, this answer does not allay the suspicion that the initial problem points towards a more general fact – that, in counting independent the predicates of (2i)–(6i), the learning-logic approach is bound to obscure relations between (2)–(6) of which a decent theory of sense should take note.

To elaborate this suspicion, consider the truth-theory K

which results if Tarski's methods are applied to a first-order language L containing the paraphrases (2i)–(6i). K, being Tarskian, will be austerely adequate, hence forms a theory of sense for L. So construed, it portrays L-speakers as having a mastery of each of (2i)–(6i) which is independent of the others, to the extent at least that mastery of no one of them guarantees mastery of any other. For K's canonical derivation of a T-sentence for a sample one of the paraphrases will invoke a special axiom dealing with the particular predicate of stabbing the sample contains; hence, it reveals that the L-speaker's capacity to assign content to the sample depends systematically upon (*inter alia*) its containing a syntactic element it shares with none of the rest, and so is a capacity which would be lacked even if the corresponding capacity as regards any of the others were possessed. But the capacity we English-speakers possess with respect to (2)–(6) is not like this; for us, as scrutiny of learners of our language is enough to attest, there are systematic interdependencies in the way we assign content, interdependencies in virtue of which mastery of (3) or (4) guarantees mastery of (2), and mastery of either (5) or (6) guarantees mastery of all the rest. K, then, may be fine as a theory of sense *for* L; but L cannot be English, nor can (2i)–(6i) be faithful enough paraphrases of the English sentences (2)–(6) to be reckoned as their base structures.

4.   The fault with the learning-logic approach is thus that it discerns too simple a structure in adverbially-adorned sentences to provide the basis of a theory of sense adequately reflecting the complexities of the systematic way in which English speakers assign contents to such sentences in primary re-description; and part at least of the diagnosis of this fault is that it fails to discern any common predicative element amongst sentences like (2)–(6). Scrutiny of the superficial grammar of these sentences immediately suggests another approach which will avoid this failing at least.

Consider (3), 'Brutus stabbed Caesar violently'. Superficial grammar suggests it is formed by combining the 2-place predicate 'Stab' with the adverb 'violently' to form a new – this time, *complex* – binary predicate, 'Stab violently', which then combines with the singular terms to yield the sentence. Or take

'Arthur slew Lancelot with Excalibur': surface grammar suggests it is formed by (i) combining 'with' with the singular term 'Excalibur' and the 2-place predicate 'Slew' to form the new, complex 2-place predicate 'Slew with Excalibur', which then (ii) combines with the singular-terms 'Arthur' and 'Lancelot' to yield the sentence. Seeking a regimenting symbolism to reflect these intuitive syntactic insights, we are led thus to the proposal that stock first-order devices be enriched by the addition of the category of *k-place predicate modifiers*: expressions which function syntactically in such a way as to combine with k terms and a predicate of some degree n to form a new predicate of the same degree. Representing 'violently' by means of the 0-place predicate modifier 'V^0' and 'with' by the 1-place modifier 'W^1', we can then render the old sample sentences (2)–(6) in the modifier symbolism like this:

(2ii) Stab(Brutus,Caesar) (= 2i)
(3ii) V^0Stab(Brutus,Caesar)
(4ii) $(\exists x)$(Knife(x) & $W^1(x)$Stab(Brutus,Caesar))
(5ii) $(\exists x)$(Knife(x) & $W^1(x)V^0$Stab(Brutus,Caesar))
(6ii) $(\exists x)$(Knife(x) & $V^0W^1(x)$Stab(Brutus,Caesar)).

Clearly, the genuine syntactic complexity of the predicates of these new paraphrases gives promise that they provide the basis for a theory of sense more adequate than the preceding proposal to reflect the niceties of the way we English-speakers handle adverbial structure. But it is hardly time yet to break out the champagne. To start with, there is the question of those entailments, previously charted, which hold between the unanalysed (2)–(6) in virtue of adverbial elimination and commutation, and which fail to hold between (2ii)–(6ii) in virtue of any standard principles of logic. To accommodate these entailments, then, new mediating principles will need to be stated – though the matter perhaps need not long detain us, since stating them is an exercise which is elementary enough. More important is the point that we have as yet a syntactic proposal merely. To fulfil its semantic promise, we still need directions for how Tarskian methods are to be extended to yield a sense-giving truth-theory for the extended first-order symbolism it proposes as that underlying adverbial English.

Certainly, there is no lack of work attempting to articulate a theory of truth for modifier-symbolism.[8] But the bulk of it is content to operate in a framework ineliminably presupposing the apparatus of possible worlds, and I gave my reasons before for thinking such apparatus has no place in a theory of truth apt for construal as a theory of sense; whereas attempts to construct a truth-theory for the modifier symbolism adequate by more austere standards, though successful perhaps for a rather exotic subclass of modifiers, seem destined to fail when the modifiers in question are ones like the homely 'violently' and 'with' of our sample sentences.[9] These considerations are, let it be granted, insufficient for rejecting the predicate-modifier approach out of hand, resting as they do on some of the more contentious of this essay's presuppositions. But they do provide motive enough in the present context for looking at it somewhat askance; and there is another and competing candidate for the treatment of adverbial structure which remains to be examined.

5. This is the treatment Davidson proposed in his classic paper, 'The Logical Form of Action Sentences'. Its leitmotif is to make first-order resources unsupplemented serve after all to accommodate adverbial structure, by exploiting a mode of first-order paraphrase more devious than that unsatisfactorily proposed by the logic learner; put briefly, its proposal is that ostensibly n-place predicates capable of adverbial adornment should be regarded as in fact $n + 1$-place, with the extra argument-place being reserved for a singular term designating an event, and that adverbs and prepositional phrases should be taken as expressing properties and relations of the events thus invoked. Applying this to the cases in hand, our first move is accordingly to add an extra event-place to the ostensibly binary predicate underlying 'stabbed'; the resulting 3-place form 'Stab(x,y,e)' we read as 'e is a stabbing by x of y', and deploying it we render the humdrum (2) ('Brutus stabbed Caesar') not along the familiar lines of (2i) but rather as the existential quantification

[8] See for example the works by Montague, by Clark, and by Thomason and Stalnaker listed in the Bibliography.
[9] See David Wiggins' 'Verbs and Adverbs', sections 5–6.

(2iii) $(\exists e)$Stab(Brutus,Caesar,e)

('some event is a stabbing by Brutus of Caesar'). The adverb 'violently' is treated now as a 1-place predicate of events, and the preposition 'with' as a 2-place predicate relating events to instruments, so that (3) ('Brutus stabbed Caesar violently') and (4) ('Brutus stabbed Caesar with a knife') are renderable as, respectively,

(3iii) $(\exists e)$(Stab(Brutus,Caesar,e) & Violent(e))

('some event is a stabbing by Brutus of Caesar, and it is violent') and

(4iii) $(\exists e)$(Stab(Brutus,Caesar,e) &
       $(\exists x)$(Knife(x) & With(x,e)))

('some event is a stabbing by Brutus of Caesar, and it is-done-with a knife'.) And putting these various elements together, the more complex adverbial structure of (5) and (6) is easily handled as well, the former going over as

(5iii) $(\exists e)$(Stab(Brutus,Caesar,e) & Violent(e) &
       $(\exists x)$(Knife(x) & With(x,e)))

and the latter as

(6iii) $(\exists e)$(Stab(Brutus,Caesar,e) & $(\exists x)$(Knife(x) &
       With(x,e)) & Violent(e)).

This Davidsonian proposal has evident virtues. To start with, entailments holding intuitively between the unanalysed (2)–(6) in virtue of adverbial elimination and commutation are reflected precisely and immediately in the paraphrases (2iii)–(6iii), being reduced to the corresponding inferences with conjunction. More importantly, in not stepping outside first-order limits, the paraphrases are amenable to a straight-forward application of Tarskian methods, yielding a theory of truth apt for construal as a theory of sense. And this time there is no reason to suspect that the constructed theory will fail to reflect the complexities of the capacity we English speakers manifest in our understanding of adverbial sentences, since the paraphrases display a satisfying predicative structure. Indeed, inspection of the theory Tarskian methods yield reveals that it accommodates *e.g.* the fact that for English-speakers, mastery of (3) or (4) guarantees mastery of (2), in an entirely natural and appealing way – in its canonical generation of T-sentences for the paraphrases (3iii) or (4iii), the theory invokes resources sufficient also to generate a T-sentence for (2iii) in canonical fashion.

6. The virtues of the Davidsonian approach just noted, are, in essence, those he observed himself in the seminal paper referred to. They do not exhaust its attraction.
    Consider

    (7) Henry gracefully ate all the crisps.

The sentence is manifestly ambiguous, having both a reading (7a) in which it requires each and every crisp to have been gracefully eaten by Henry, but also a construal (7b) which requires only overall grace in Henry's crisp-eating style, compatible with graceless devoural of the odd crisp. And it is a further apparent merit of Davidson's proposal that it contains the apparatus to explicate this ambiguity, by interpeting (7) as either (7a) predicating gracefulness of each of Henry's individual crisp-eatings, or else (7b) predicating gracefulness rather of an event formed by summing these individual crisp-eatings to obtain a further crisp-eating of Henry's, his eating-of-all-the-crisps.

    To be sure, there is a finesse involved in translating this thought into the symbolism. One's first impulse is (my first impulse was) to do so by rendering (7) in its first sense (7a) into Davidsonian formalism as

    (7ai) $(\forall y)(\text{Crisp}(y) \rightarrow (\exists e)(\text{Eat}(\text{Henry},y,e)$ &
          $\text{Graceful}(e)))$

('for each crisp, there is an eating by Henry of that crisp and it is graceful') and in its (7b) construal to paraphrase it as

    (7bi) $(\exists e)((\forall y)(\text{Crisp}(y) \rightarrow \text{Eat}(\text{Henry},y,e))$ &
          $\text{Graceful}(e))$

('there is an event which is an eating by Henry of all the crisps, and it is graceful'). But this first impulse won't do, since – as Harry Lewis pointed out to me – by predicate logic it makes reading (7b) *entail* (7a), as it manifestly does not. The remedy is to be more careful in the rendering of (7a): let

Eat(x, y uniquely, e)

abbreviate

Eat(x,y,e) & ($\forall z$)(Eat(x,z,e) → $z = y$)

and then for (7ai) substitute

(7ai′) ($\forall y$)(Crisp(y) → (∃e)(Eat(Henry, y uniquely, e) & Graceful(e)))

('for each crisp, there is an eating by Henry of that crisp alone, and it is graceful').

Davidson's apparatus thus neatly handles the ambiguity of (7), even if some care is needed in putting its insights into symbols. By contrast, the competing predicate-modifier approach – waiving, for the moment, doubts already expressed about its general semantic adequacy – can accommodate the case only with difficulty. It has, of course, no problem with sense (7a) of (7), which it can render just as

(7aii) ($\forall y$)(Crisp(y) → (G^0Eat(Henry,y)))

where 'G^0' regiments 'gracefully'. But to handle sense (7b), it has no evident choice but to complicate its syntactic proposal so as to allow that *complex* predicates (formed, say, by λ-abstraction) as well as simple ones can fall within the scope of predicate-modifiers, so that sense (7b) can go over as

(7bii) G^0(λx)[($\forall y$)(Crisp(y) → Eat(x,y))] Henry).

This special extension to cover the vagaries of (7) is ugly, contrasting unfavourably with the smooth Davidsonian handling of the same phenomena; and, by invoking a further extension to first order resources, can only add to semantic difficulties the predicate-modifier approach already faces. It engenders, moreover, further problems.

For consider now

(8) *Brutus violently did not stab Caesar.

As the awarded asterisk indicates, the sentence fails to make coherent sense, and we should expect of a proper semantics an explanation of its deviance. This the Davidsonian approach evidently supplies, just by failing to make sense of (8) by providing it with a base structure – for however a negation-sign is inserted into its paraphrase (3iii) of 'Brutus violently stabbed Caesar', the result makes construable sense short of the nonsense of (8). But the predicate-modifier theory, forced as it has been by the ambiguity of (7) into admitting complex predicates into the scope of modifiers, must acknowledge the existence of a form

(8i) $V^0(\lambda x)\,[\sim\!\text{Stab}(x,\text{Caesar})]\,(\text{Brutus})$

which clearly mirrors the deviant (8); and hence is faced with the task of explaining how (8), though receiving well-formed paraphrase into its preferred base symbolism, should nevertheless ultimately be judged incoherent.

7. The Davidsonian explanation of the deviance of (8) generalizes, of course, to all sentences of the same form; and here there may seem to be grounds for objection. For, the deviance of (8) itself notwithstanding, the apparently equiform

(9a) Brutus intentionally did not stab Caesar.
(9b) Brutus voluntarily did not stab Caesar

are entirely unexceptionable. Which suggests the modifier-theorist may be on firm ground after all in eschewing a *formal* diagnosis of (8)'s failings, and that Davidson's proposal may suffer from a serious undersupply of base structures (since in refusing to supply a form to underpin the deviant (8), it cuts itself off from accommodating the acceptable (9a) and (9b)).

Davidson has, of course, a response to this objection ready. For his paper makes it perfectly clear that he never intended his analysis to extend to the 'intentionally' and 'voluntarily' of (9a) and (9b) – these, as adverbs which (as he puts it) 'impute intention',[10] are to be treated in some way quite other than as event-predicates, a way whose discovery will he predicts emerge out of a solution to the general problem of the analysis of sentences ascribing propositional attitudes. The structural

[10] See 'Logical Form', p. 82.

similarity of the deviant (8) and the acceptable (9a) and (9b) is thus by Davidson's lights a matter merely of superficial grammar, and his account can happily regard the former as formally incoherent whilst deploying further and quite distinct (if yet-to-be-discovered) resources in supplying base structures for the latter pair.

The response is plausible, and serves as a salutary reminder that my description, back at the start of section 2, of the present essay's principal concern as being with the complexities engendered for the theory of sense by 'adverbial constructions' may need some refinement and revision, since it cannot be too hastily assumed that the adverbial constructions recognized by schoolboy grammar form a unitary semantic class. Still, this Davidsonian response does raise the question of whether it is really satisfactory merely to characterize the adverbs his treatment excludes as those which 'impute intention'. Granted, it is unreasonable to demand more than a rough and ready prior characterization of the intended scope of this or any other proposal for semantic analysis, since typically in such cases precision can be achieved only by using the resources the proposal itself implements. But a moment's reflection is enough to reveal that there are many adverbs ('necessarily', 'allegedly') which resist Davidsonian treatment whilst in no way 'imputing intention', and others with which the analysis sits uneasily and which, though perhaps in some tenuous ways related to intention, by no means directly impute it ('inadvertently', 'mistakenly'). It is fair to ask for a speci-fication, however roughly stated, of more definite limits to the legitimate range of Davidson's proposal.

To which end, let me distinguish (a) *sentence adverbs* – *i.e.*, those adverbs M which permit natural rewording of contexts of the form 'x φ-ed M-ly' as 'it was M that x φ-ed'; (b) *phrase adverbs*, which permit rephrasing of similar contexts as 'it was M of x that x φ-ed'; and (c) *mode adverbs*, which fit neither previous category. Then the suggestion is that only adverbs of the last sort form the proper domain of Davidsonian analysis, the other two types requiring some special treatment whose details remain to be settled. This suggestion has the virtue at least of agreeing with Davidson's own explicit exclusions – *e.g.* 'intentionally' and 'voluntarily' emerge as phrase adverbs; and also of excluding the obviously unsuitable 'necessarily' and 'allegedly', which are ruled sentential. But there is a complexity involved in using it to decide just when an adverb falls positively *within* the Davidsonian scope.

This is the phenomenon of *Austinian ambiguity.* For Austin noted[11] a characteristic ambiguity of many adverbs enabling them to function, in the present terminology, as adverbs either of phrase or of mode. Thus 'he deliberately ate his soup' may according to Austin mean 'that his eating his soup was a deliberate act' (and so be rephrasable as 'it was deliberate of him that he ate his soup', classifying the adverb as of phrase variety), or 'that he went through the performance of eating his soup in a deliberate manner or *style* – pause after each mouthful, careful choice of point of entry for spoon' (and so resist canonical rewording, rendering the adverb on this construal one of mode). And 'he clumsily trod on the snail' may as Austin noted either 'describe his treading on the creature at all as a piece of clumsiness' and – being then rewordable as 'it was clumsy of him that he trod on the snail' – display the adverb in a phrase sense; or else may be used to criticize not the fact of his action but 'his execution of the feat', and use the adverb in a mode sense. (Austin also thought the phrase sense more to the fore when the adverb precedes rather than follows its verb. Presumably this is because the earlier positioning is more suggestive of the rewording characteristic of the phrase adverb.) A plethora of examples join Austin's paradigms; 'modestly', 'impatiently', 'casually', 'impetuously', 'irascibly', ...[12] In some instances the phrase adverb sense is generally the more obvious, in others the mode meaning predominates; in all cases it is in its mode sense alone that an adverb falls properly within the range of Davidson's proposal.

The delineation of that range just given applies moreover best to *simple* adverbs only – for the suggested taxonomy applied neat to the bulk of prepositional phrases would rule them sentential (since *e.g.* 'Brutus stabbed Caesar with a knife'

[11] 'A Plea for Excuses', pp. 198–200.
[12] Amongst them are the 'violently' and 'gracefully' of earlier paradigm sentences, which should accordingly be re-read as intending the adverb in its mode sense only. But note that the relevant ambiguity of (7) survives this re-interpretation.

rewords neatly as 'It was with a knife that Brutus stabbed Caesar') and hence exclude them unnecessarily from the Davidsonian domain. As a remedy, I suggest complicating the definition of sentence adverbs, so as to require that they should not only permit the rewording of 'x φ-ed M-ly' as 'it was M that x φ-ed', but should also be such that the rewording displays terms following 'it was M that' as occupying referentially opaque position. Then 'allegedly', *e.g.*, remains sentential, because in rewording 'Ortcutt is allegedly a spy' as 'it is alleged that Ortcutt is a spy' the position the singular term occupies is opaque; but 'with a knife' by the revised standard eludes classification as sentential and consequent exclusion from the Davidsonian range, since the rewording of my favourite sentence about Brutus, Caesar and that knife still displays all singular terms as occurring in referentially transparent place. Indeed, most prepositional phrases will emerge from the new test as complex, nonsentential, mode adverbs – but not all, *e.g.* 'for John's sake'.

The finesse just employed in stretching my taxonomical criteria so as to fit prepositional phrases into the right box suggests indeed that there may be a cleaner way of marking off mode adverbs from both their sentential and their phrase-adverb colleagues. For typically phrase adverbs too are such that when sentences containing them are reworded, singular-terms are displayed as occupying opaque position. (Rephrasing 'Oedipus intentionally married Jocasta' as 'it was intentional of Oedipus that he married Jocasta' clearly displays the position of 'Jocasta' as nontransparent.) So we might suggest that the mark of the non-mode adverb is that it permits a rephrasing which displays singular-terms in opaque position, whilst mode adverbs are those which never generate opacities. But, while the idea is attractive, I am not entirely confident that *all* phrase adverbs do indeed generate opacities in the way the suggestion requires, my misgivings centring primarily upon the phrase adverb sense of Austinianly-ambiguous adverbs where the mode adverb sense is to the fore. 'Clumsily' is a case in point; when it takes its phrase-adverb sense, 'He clumsily trod on the snail' rephrases as 'it was clumsy of him that he trod on the snail', but it is not obvious that any singular-term position in the rewording is nontransparent.

But I do not wish to bog down in classificatory niceties, nor is there any need for me to do so; for I was under contract only to supply a rough and intuitive account of the intended scope of Davidson's analysis, and have given one which may fairly claim to improve significantly on Davidson's own. It is enough to establish in particular that Davidson's proposal takes as its range a class of adverbial structures naturally distinguished from the rest by preanalytic intuition, rendering less than arbitrary Davidson's diagnosis that (9a) and (9b) despite superficial grammatical similarities differ in form from the deviant (8). What *would*, on the present account, prove trouble for the Davidsonian line would be production of an acceptable sentence of the form 'x M-ly did not φ' where M was an uncontroversial adverb of *mode*. But reflection on the fact that *e.g.* (9a) remains acceptable if 'deliberately' is put for 'intentionally' only when the ambiguous adverb is taken in its phrase sense adds to the conviction that there are no such sentences to be produced.

8.　I am sufficiently impressed by the distinctions into which I was forced in the discussion of the last section to suspect that adverbial constructions as identified by schoolboy grammar do not form a unitary semantic class. Even if the generation of referential opacity is not a *decisive* litmus of the phrase or sentence adverb, it is clear at least that a proper account of adverbs of these classes is going to impinge on the topic of intentionality; whereas mode adverbs on the face of it remain independent of that messy and much-discussed issue. And when I said, back at the start of section 2, that I wanted to concentrate on the problems raised for the theory of sense by adverbial constructions, I had in mind a class of problems which adverbial structure seems to raise in its purest form, problems isolable from those inherent in other devices in our language. These now seem to be describable more precisely as those raised by *mode* adverbs, complex and simple. So it is on adverbs of this sort only that I shall from henceforth concentrate. And so far Davidson's theory seems well ahead of its main rival, the predicate-modifier theory, as an account of mode adverbs – not only because it can get by without invoking the dubious apparatus of possible worlds, but also because it seems structurally superior, being able with relative ease to accommodate both the ambiguity of (7) and the deviance of (8).

But the semantic insights of Davidson's proposal are purchased, of course, at the ontological expense of quantifying over events. Now it would be metaphysically churlish to take exception to these simply on the ground that they diverge from some cherished paradigm of the really real – bricks, electrons, or sensations; for the fact, if it is one, that invoking events brings the best explanation for puzzling features of language is reason enough for over-riding metaphysical prejudice. (If this ontological tolerance seems ill to become one who has objected to a semantic proposal, the predicate-modifier theory, in part on the ground that it invokes the apparatus of possible worlds, recall that my objection to that apparatus is not ontological, but rather that its invocation brings only dubious semantic insight from the standpoint of the theory of sense properly construed.) And for similar reasons, there is no justification for requiring *a priori* that events be reduced to items of some more familiar sort, and Davidson has rightly refused to bend to any such demand. Still, no dubious motivation is required to ask questions about events which seem to need an answer: When is event e_1 literally the same as event e_2? How do events relate to substances – what relation does Brutus bear to his stabbing of Caesar? How do events relate one to the other – what relation obtains between Henry's eating of some one crisp and his eating of the lot? (Could it be the same as the relation between Brutus and his stabbing?) And what *kinds* of events in general exist? To answer these questions is to give a *theory* of events; such a theory need not of its nature be reductionist, but may like set-theory aim merely to map the features of entities it assumes irreducible using minimal primitive ideology – though reductionism would be justified if motivated, not by prior prejudice alone, but by the theory's own internal demands.

The need for a theory thus explicating the nature of events is not a matter merely of expiating a conscience which over-nicely aims at leaving no metaphysical stone unturned. Rather, it forms an integral part of a proper articulation of Davidson's adverbial proposals. For those proposals depend in large part for their explanatory power on the controversial assumption that the true event-theory will take a certain shape. Thus, the account of the ambiguity of (7) requires that the underlying theory allows that events sometimes sum to yield a further and distinct one; yet the idea requires further elaboration and defence, since intuition baulks at the notion that such summing is universally permissible (there is surely no one event comprising both Lennon's death and Charles's wedding). Again, the explanation of the deviance of (8) depends on the assumption that the right event-theory will countenance no such event as Brutus' not stabbing Caesar; for were such an event to exist, the failure of Davidsonian symbolism to provide a form to underpin (8) would show only the deficiency of the formalism. A less-than-naive theory of events is thus inchoately embodied in Davidson's adverbial proposals, and its systematic elaboration should form an essential part of their evaluation.

Yet Davidson himself can hardly be claimed to have attempted such an elaboration, perhaps because – not having pushed his own account to consideration of sentences like (7) and (8), with their attendant complications for event-theory – he saw no motivation for the demand for it beyond meta-physical puritanism or *a priori* reductionism. Indeed, his sole explicit gesture towards theory-building consists in his suggestion of the criterion of event-identity, that e_1 is e_2 just in case e_1 and e_2 share all causes and effects,[13] and it is not entirely clear that this criterion jibes well with his adverbial proposals. For, as Davidson notes, if Susan crossed the Channel by swimming it, the criterion rules her Channel-swimming identical with her Channel-crossing; but, since she may have crossed slowly whilst swimming quickly, this identity means that 'quickly' and 'slowly' cannot be treated as straightforwardly predicating quickness and slowness of events. Well aware of this problem, Davidson assimilates 'quickly' and 'slowly' to attributive adjectives in the category of substance – just as 'big' describes things not outright but only after a kind (as big-for-mice or big-for-animals), so 'quick' and 'slow' describe events only relative to an event-sort (as quick-for-Channel-swimmings or slow-for-

---

[13] See 'The Individuation of Events'.

Channel-crossings); and goes on to exclude these and other 'attributive adverbs' from the scope of his main analysis, to await discovery of a satisfactory treatment for attributives generally. It is reasonable, perhaps, that if adverbs are to be assimilated to adjectives, a class of attributive adverbs should emerge. What is more problematic is whether *Davidson's* attributive adverbs form a preanalytically natural class, or whether they are an artefact rather of welding a mismatched identity-criterion onto his adverbial proposals.

'Quickly' and 'slowly', maybe, are sound candidates for attributive status, given their connexions with the phrases 'in a short time' and 'in a long time', and the uncontroversially attributive nature of 'short' and 'long'. But other cases generate less plausible examples. Thus (to use a case I owe to Christopher Arnold), Oswald's killing of Kennedy is by Davidson's standards identical with his pulling of the trigger; but Oswald killed Kennedy with a rifle; so if the unacceptable conclusion that Oswald pulled the trigger with a rifle is to be avoided, complex mode adverbs formed by means of the humble 'with' must join the attributive pariahs. And a case given by David Wiggins,[14] in which a walking uphill is by Davidson's criterion also a warning, seems to indicate that a similar fate awaits 'uphill'. The attributive adverbs generated by Davidson's identity criterion are a motley crew, with the appearance of no motive for assembly save the *ad hoc* demands of theory.

9. It follows from the foregoing that the structural insights of Davidson's adverbial proposals require underpinning by a theory of events with the complexity necessary to sustain them; and that such a theory must in particular be one that allows for discriminate summing of events to form further ones, whilst refusing to countenance such negative events as Brutus' not-stabbing of Caesar (and being under no evident obligation to follow Davidson himself in the matter of identity criteria). What might the desired theory look like?

Giving one answer to that question will be the main task of the bulk of the succeeding pages. In giving it, I will range well

[14] See Wiggins' 'Verbs and Adverbs', section 13.

away from the adverbial concerns of this chapter, and deploy apparatus which may seem ill-suited to a work which aims ultimately to be answerable to the austere demands of the theory of sense. But once the nature of events has been clarified, I shall return in my final chapter to the themes of this one.

2

States of Affairs

1. Philosophers as diverse as the Johns Austin and Anderson have deployed the apparatus of 'facts' and 'states of affairs' in formulating their key tenets; and the notions are firmly entrenched in our philosophical heritage not only because there are theorists like these – and Russell, Moore, and the early Wittgenstein, to name but a few – who have invoked them in the most self-conscious of ways in elaborating their doctrines, but also because they have been found natural and convenient ones to use by a host of other philosophers in a more casual articulation of theory. Of course, divergent philosophers disagree (often vehemently) in the minutiae of the apparatus thus invoked, as in the terminology they find most appropriate to describe it. But, enshrining one terminology as canonical, it seems fair to describe the core of the teaching of the tradition like this: states of affairs are things in the world with which sentences (closed formulae) are correlated (we shall say a sentence *describes* its correlated state of affairs). More specifically, the state of affairs which a sentence describes is a 'logical complex' having as its 'constituents' the entities which are relevant for that sentence's truth. Some states of affairs, moreover, have an interesting property – they *obtain*. Such states of affairs are *facts*; and a sentence is true just in case the state of affairs it describes is a fact.

The (less than original) leading idea of my conception of events is that they are best thought of as a species of states of affairs, or, more precisely, as a species of facts. And my goal in this chapter is to present a precise set-theoretic construction of states of affairs, so as to be clear at least on the nature of the genus to which, I maintain, events belong.

2.   Evidently, such a construction might go one of two ways. One would be to define a totality of entities claimed to provide a stock of descripta adequate for the demands of any language whatsoever; in that case, given any language short of some idealized universal one, there will presumably be some states of affairs in the defined totality whose obtaining or otherwise is irrelevant to the truth-values of sentences of the language. Alternatively, each language L might be regarded as bringing with it its own conception of a totality of states of affairs – the states of affairs, as we may say, *posited by L*, the obtaining or otherwise of any of which has some ramifications for the truth-values of L-sentences; and the major task for a theory embodying this second conception would be that of describing a general method whereby, given a language L, we might construct the set of states of affairs which it posits. The second approach is the one to be adopted here, and to keep the material within manageable limits I shall concentrate on the case where L is first-order (a focusing of interest unlikely to prove too restrictive in applying the construction in the present context, given the assumption of the last chapter that the base structures of English are first-order at the core). So the task of the present chapter becomes that of describing a general method whereby, given first-order L, the states of affairs posited by L may be constructed.

3.   What criteria should be met by a formal construction which can reasonably claim to explicate traditional views about states of affairs? Let us say that sentences S and S' of L are *chainwise connected* if S' is obtainable from S by (i) replacing sentences by their logical equivalents and (ii) substituting co-referring singular terms within sentences. (To put it more formally: let $S(t_2//t_1)$ be the result of putting a term t_2 of L for *some* free occurrence of another such term t_1 in a sentence S of L. Then sentences S and S' are chainwise connected just in case there is a sequence $S_1 \ldots S_n$ of L-

sentences $(n>0)$ such that $S_1 = S$, $S_n = S'$, and for each $i(1 \leqslant i < n)$, either (i) S_i is logically equivalent to S_{i+1} or (ii) S_{i+1} is $S_i(t_2//t_1)$, for some co-referring terms t_1 and t_2.) Then it seems that to ensure a reasonable correspondence with traditional views, we should require at least of a theory of the states of affairs posited by L that it should define a set Σ of entities, a predicate of *obtaining*, and a relation of *description*, meeting the following conditions:

[Condition 1] Each sentence of L describes a unique element of Σ

[Condition 2] Sentences of L which are chainwise connected describe the same element of Σ

[Condition 3] If an element of Σ is described by a sentence of L, then the element obtains just in case the describing sentence is true.

For Conditions 1 and 3 apparently just enshrine fundamental features of states of affairs as traditionally conceived – that they are descripta of sentences, and that the descripta of true sentences differ crucially from the descripta of false ones. And Condition 2 embodies two further evident consequences of the traditional conception of the descriptum of a sentence as the complex of the entities relevant for its truth – that sentences so closely connected as to be guaranteed by logic alone to share a truth-value cannot differ in truth-relevant entities, and so must share their descriptum; and that sentences which, like 'Cicero orated' and 'Tully orated', differ merely in the manner they choose to specify the *same* truth-relevant entity cannot diverge in the complex of such entities they describe.

Not that Conditions 1–3 embody the traditional conception of the state of affairs in its full richness. For the theorists of the past who made fullest use of the notion felt free to deploy the distinctions and concepts of intensional semantics with a robustness which cannot properly be shared by minds now sicklied o'er with the paler cast of Quinean thought, and I have thought it best to state my conditions in a way which does not commit the construction we envisage to reflecting those features of classical views which presuppose outright the viability of concepts now suspect. Indeed, Condition 1 is actually directly at odds with one very common thesis of the tradition – that synthetic sentences alone describe states of affairs, analytic sentences lacking genuine descriptive power. (*Cf. e.g.* Wittgenstein in the *Tractatus* at 4.462: 'Tautologies . . . do not represent any possible situations', and combine this with his view that all analyticities are at bottom tautologies.) Still, the stated conditions do end up throwing a considerable sop to this scepticism in the tradition regarding the descriptive powers of purportedly analytic sentences, since Condition 2 guarantees at least that that important subset of those sentences which even Quine regards as distinguished, *viz* the logical truths, are limited to trivial possession of the same descriptum.

Intensional terminology is implicit too in two other theses commonly espoused in the tradition: the negative thesis that *e.g.* the mere co*extensiveness* of the contained predicates is *in*sufficient to guarantee that 'Quine is cordate' and 'Quine is renate' describe the same state of affairs; and the positive thesis that the co*intensiveness* or synonymy of the contained predicates *does* guarantee the uniqueness of descriptum of such pairs of sentences as 'Alfred is an aardvark' and 'Alfred is a groundhog'. (*Cf.* Russell's view in *The Philosophy of Logical Atomism*, p. 53 that the predicative component of the simplest sort of fact is an intensionally-differentiated *quality.*) The latter thesis in particular suggests that Condition 2 might more faithfully reflect the tradition if the notion of chainwise connexion it embodies were extended so as to allow a link in the connecting chain to be forged by substituting a synonymous primitive predicate for a similar predicate occurring in the preceding chain-member. To avoid outright commitment to the intensional, my conditions fall short of imposing this extended requirement; though this time they are not so far at odds with the tradition as to require that an explication meeting them should actually flout it.

Modulo reservations about the intensional, can we take it accordingly that a reasonable explication of the apparatus of states of affairs will be provided by a theory meeting Conditions 1–3? – *i.e.*, can we take it that any theory meeting these conditions will reasonably explicate at least that core of the traditional doctrine of states of affairs which escapes Quinean censure? No, for they are too trivially met. (Take Σ as the set of all sets of L-sentences, define the descriptum of a sentence S of L as the set of all L-sentences to which S is chainwise connected, and construe an element of Σ as obtaining iff all of its members are true.) Conditions 1–3 must be regarded as embodying the *structural* criteria only which a purified theory of states of affairs should fulfil; to be acceptable, such a theory must also meet a condition of *material* adequacy – the elements of Σ which it construes as states of affairs must recognizably be, in a sense which the theory itself must make precise, complexes whose constituents are the truth-relevant entities of the sentences which describe them. The present chapter's task thus becomes that of describing a method whereby, given first-order L, a theory of the states of affairs posited by L may be constructed which is materially adequate and which meets the structural Conditions 1–3. (And if, of course, the constructed theory manages respectably to incorporate features of the traditional views beyond those actually demanded by these cautiously-worded conditions, so much the better.)

4.   Yet it has been claimed persistently in the recent literature, most loudly by Davidson,[1] that there are formal results which render the present chapter's aims as just stated quite nugatory. For the concentration in those stated aims on first-order language is intended of course primarily as a matter of expository convenience only, with the assumption that a method which worked to produce a satisfactory theory for given first-order L would, with appropriate extension, work too if L were stretched by the addition of some intuitively motivated and formally tractable non-first-order device. One simple way to extend first-order resources is to add to them a primitive operator for forming definite descriptions (let us write it as 'I', and with Dana Scott[2] regard our symbol as an inversion of the normal Roman capital, reminding us of Russell's inverted iota), and we should accordingly expect of

_____

[1] See *e.g.* 'True to the Facts', pp. 752–3; 'Truth and Meaning', p. 306; 'Causal Relations', pp. 694–5. See also the papers by Anscombe and Morton given in the Bibliography.

[2] See his 'Existence and Description', p. 182.

any construction applicable to purely first-order L that it should be extendible to deal with $L + I$. But, the claim is, this is not on: formal results show that no theory of states of affairs for a first-order language enriched with a primitive definite description operator can be materially adequate and meet the structural Conditions 1–3.

But the formal results upon which this claim purports to rest need some examination, especially as the invocation of them in the literature has had a somewhat hand-waving air. The key result relied upon (in the claim's most respectable formulation) would seem to be this:

> [Main Result.] Where L is a first-order language enriched with a primitive description operator, then any two true sentences S and S' of L are chainwise connected.

And this does look worrying. For chainwise-connected sentences must, in a theory meeting Condition 2, describe the same state of affairs; yet an arbitrary pair of true sentences need intuitively share no truth-relevant entity, so will be made in a materially adequate theory of states of affairs to describe distinct complexes; so that the Main Result looks to establish that no theory of states of affairs can apply to a language with a primitive description operator and be adequate both structurally and materially. Moreover, the Main Result appears to have a convincing proof: for where S and S' are true sentences of L, and 'a' is some individual constant of L, the sequence

(i) S
(ii) $a = (Ix)(x = a \ \& \ S)$
(iii) $a = (Ix)(x = a \ \& \ S')$
(iv) S'

evidently establishes the chainwise-connectedness of S and S' which the problem result claims. (For (i) and (ii) are logically equivalent, as are (iii) and (iv). And (iii) is (ii) $((Ix)(x = a \ \& \ S')//(Ix)(x = a \ \& \ S))$, where the assumed truth of both S and S' ensures that the two descriptions co-refer.)

A friend of states of affairs, perturbed by this Main Result, might be tempted to take consolation from the fact that its proof makes essential use of 'odd' definite descriptions which, like '$(Ix)(x = a \ \& \ S)$', contain in their matrix a conjunct with no free variable to be bound by the operator-variable of the description; and then attempt to avoid his problems by in some way restricting the notion of chainwise connectedness so as not to allow such odd definite descriptions to count as establishing that such a connexion holds. But that rabbit won't run, since there is apparently a second result in the offing:

> [Subsidiary Result.] Let L be a first-order language enriched with a primitive definite description operator, and let A and B be true sentences of L respectively containing singular terms 'a' and 'b'. Then these sentences are chainwise connected.

This result is as disconcerting for the advocate of states of affairs as was its predecessor, but is apparently provable without recourse to odd definite descriptions. For A and B are it seems chainwise-connected in virtue of the sequence

(i') A
(ii') $a = (Ix)(x = a \ \& \ A(x//a))$
(iii') $a = a$
(iv') $b = b$
(v') $b = (Ix)(x = b \ \& \ B(x//b))$
(vi') B.

(For (i') and (ii') are logically equivalent, as are (v') and (vi'); and as too are (iii') and (iv'), since both are logical truths. And (iii') is just (ii') $(a//(Ix)(x = a \ \& \ A(x//a))$, where the terms are guaranteed co-referring by the truth of A; and (v') comes from (iv') symmetrically.)

5. But before becoming too perturbed by these formal results, we should note that their proofs are invalid on at least one theory of the way primitive description operators work.

A key notion invoked in the structural conditions we have imposed is that of logical equivalence, a notion whose proper explication awaits clarification of the more general notion of logical truth (sentences S and S' being logically equivalent iff a biconditional linking them is logically true). And explication of logical truth for L is the task undertaken by a *model-theory for L*: a theory which defines a class of structures (the 'models for L') and which assigns, relative to any given model, truth-values to L-sentences recursively dependent upon model-relative assignments of appropriate semantic values to their primitive parts; and then defines a logical truth of L as one which turns out true relative to all of its models. (Of an adequate model-theory, we should accordingly require at least that the set of L-sentences it rules to be logical truths should intuitively be so describable; and it is hard to see how it could do this without there being some systematic connexion between the concept of model-relative truth it embodies and the intuitive notion of truth *simpliciter* – a connexion it can in self-justification articulate if it can designate some model as a distinguished one, truth relative to which is truth *simpliciter*.) Now, call a definite description '$(Ix)A(x)$' of L *standard* (according to some model M) iff its matrix '$A(x)$' is on M's interpretation true of just one element in the domain D_M over which M regards L's variables as ranging; and *rotten* (according to M) if M interprets the matrix as true of no elements of D_M, or of more than one.[3] Then evidently any reasonable model-theory is constrained by elementary and noncontroversial features of the intuitive meaning of the description operator to treat a standard description in M as designating in M (having as its semantic value in M) that unique element of D_M of which the matrix is true. But intuition does not so clearly dictate what model-theory should do with rotten descriptions, and different versions of model-theory diverge in their treatment of these defective cases.

One model-theoretic way with rotten description is Frege's: a convention is laid down whereby a description rotten on M is counted more or less arbitrarily as designating in M some element of D_M, the only constraint on an acceptable convention being extensionality – that it should construe rotten descriptions whose embedded matrices are coextensive on M as designating the *same* element of D_M. (In its simplest form, a Fregean model-theory might accordingly embody a con-

---

[3] The alternatives are not exclusive, since the matrix '$A(x)$' can contain free variables. They can, of course, be made exclusive if relativized to variable-assignments (sequences), but I prefer in this section to skirt the irrelevant complexities which over-concentration on the niceties of free variables brings.

vention singling out, for each model M, some unfortunate element of D_M to function as the denotation in M of all descriptions M rules rotten. Or, if the domains D_M are set-theoretically closed, a more sophisticated convention might make a description rotten on M designate the whole *set* of elements of D_M of which the matrix it embeds is true.) Now if our model-theory for the description-operator takes this Fregean form, then the arguments given for the Main and Subsidiary Results of the last section fail to work. For the argument for the Main Result claimed a logical equivalence between

(i) S

and (ii) $a = (\mathrm{I}x)(x = a \,\&\, S)$

which does not hold on a Fregean account, since a Fregean model M which counts S false and treats 'a' as designating in M that element of D_M which is conventionally assigned as the designation of rotten descriptions whose matrix has the null extension will be one in which (ii) is true though (i) is false. And for precisely similar reasons the equivalence between (iii) and (iv), upon which the 'proof' of the Main Result also depends, fails too within a Fregean framework; as also do the equivalences between (i') and (ii'), and (v') and (vi'), urged in the 'proof' of the Subsidiary Result.

At this point a defender of the Main and Subsidiary Results might retort that they have been impugned from the perspective of Fregean model-theory only, and urge that such a model-theory is really of very little interest, certainly having no bearing on a description-operator which can reasonably be claimed to regiment the definite article of English – for there is no way of designating a model of a Fregean model-theory relative to which Fregean descriptions have semantic properties shared too by English descriptions they might claim to regiment, since there is just no intuitively motivated answer to the question of what things rotten descriptions in English denote. Still, this response will not quite do. For there are more sophisticated versions of Fregean model-theory proposed by Scott and Grandy,[4] which allow the denotations of rotten

---

[4] See the works by these authors listed in the Bibliography.

descriptions to be 'quasi-objects' drawn from beyond a model's normal quantificational domain, and Grandy has argued persuasively that his version in particular can claim neatly to reflect the intuitive properties of unregimented English; and on both of these treatments too the crucial logical equivalences used to establish the Main and Subsidiary Results fail, provided only that individual constants are like definite descriptions permitted to denote quasi-objects.[5] Indeed, so far as I can see, only one of the model-theoretic treatments current in the literature *does* succeed in validating these logical equivalences. This is the Strawsonian one,[6] which forsaking bivalence counts sentences containing a definite description rotten in some model as lacking truth-value entirely in that model, and reckons as logically equivalent any pair of sentences which share the same truth-value in every model in which both have any truth-value at all. (To see that (i) and (ii) emerge as logical equivalents on such a model-theory, reflect that the falsity of (i) in a model M suffices for the rottenness in M of the description in (ii), and so for the failure of (ii) itself to possess truth-value in M. So if (ii) possesses truth-value in M, (i) is true in M. But, further, though (ii) may lack truth-value altogether in some models, it can never be false in a model. So if (i) and (ii) jointly possess a truth-value at all in any model, both are true; hence they are Strawsonian logical equivalents. And similar considerations establish the rest of our crucial equivalences.) Apparently then, the Main and Subsidiary Results held to threaten the construction of states of affairs this chapter envisages depend upon the controversial thesis that the One True Model-Theory goes Strawson's way.

6. But perhaps, after all, it does. And even if it doesn't, there are ways of adapting the Main and Subsidiary Results so that

[5] Thus in Scott's treatment the equivalence of (i) and (ii) is once more refuted by a model which falsifies S but assigns to 'a' the element denoted by descriptions whose matrix has the null extension. In Grandy's case, the assignment to 'a' will be the element denoted by all descriptions whose matrix has the *intension* of '$x = a$ & S'. Corresponding countermodels refute the other relevant 'equivalences'.

[6] Obtained by reproducing in model-theoretic terms the views expressed in Strawson's 'On Referring'.

they really do apply even within a Fregean model-theory, and still pose headaches for the friend of states of affairs. Thus, take this

> [Modified Main Result.] Where L is a first-order language enriched with a primitive definite-description operator, S and S' are any two true sentences of L, and 'a' any individual constant of L, then the sentences
> $$S \mathbin{\&} a \neq (\mathrm{I}x)(x \neq x)$$
> and $\quad S' \mathbin{\&} a \neq (\mathrm{I}x)(x \neq x)$
> are chainwise connected.

To prove it, take the same sequence (i)–(iv) as the original Main Result appealed to, and tack on '$a \neq (\mathrm{I}x)(x \neq x)$' as a conjunct to each; then the constructed sequence establishes the chainwise-connectedness the modified Result claims, and this time appeals to no logical equivalences to which even Fregean model-theory objects. Yet it is just as worrying as its unmodified predecessor, since just as no materially adequate conception of states of affairs can tolerate the idea that 'Socrates was wise' and 'Carnap was a positivist' are co-descriptive, no more can it accept that they become so if encumbered with the conjunct 'Thatcher is not the non-self-identical object'. (And, to hammer the point here, a similar adjustment will suffice to produce a Frege-proof modified version of the Subsidiary Result as well.)

All of which may seem just to return us to a point reached some time back, that there are formal results posing problems for a theory of states of affairs meeting our conditions, and so make seem rather pointless the last section's discursion on the niceties of model-theory and logical truth. But we are not quite back where we started. For the last section serves at least to highlight the murkier aspects of the primitive description operator, and demonstrates the involvement of the threatening formal results with that operator's less-than-perspicuous properties, since the obtainable results vary sensitively with the finer detail of its semantic treatment.

That in turn suggests a way out of the present problem. Quine has emphasized how the notion of logical truth is vague, depending on what he calls a 'prior inventory' of particles singled out as logical (and, in model-theoretic explication, held constant in their interpretation from model to model). And that vagueness carries over into our structural conditions, via Condition 2's invocation of logical equivalence as a mode of generating chainwise connexion. The obvious move, then, is to restate Condition 2 more sharply, making it clear that its appeal to logical equivalence is to a notion which does not account the description operator amongst logical vocabulary, and rendering it immune from formal results which construe the notion more widely. Accordingly, I propose we define as a *tight* logical truth one which so counts when quantifiers and truth-functional connectives alone are counted amongst logical vocabulary, and reconstrue Condition 2 as Condition $2^{\#}$ – that form of the condition which results when the notion of chainwise connectedness is replaced by that of *tight* chainwise connectedness (chainwise connectedness in which all logical equivalences in the connecting chain are tight). To be sure, this sharper reformulation of Condition 2 is stricter than it need be, since to disqualify the sequences (i)–(iv) or (i′)–(vi′) as establishing tight chainwise connectedness it would be sufficient to operate with a notion of tight logical equivalence which excluded *either* the description-operator *or* the identity predicate from the favoured inventory of logical particles, whereas the present proposal is to exclude both. But the two devices are so intimately connected (as Russell demonstrated in showing how identity alone already achieved so much of what the primitive description operator attempts to add) that it seems idle to attempt to find a restriction which will favour the one at the expense of the other.

Finally stated, then, this chapter's task becomes that of giving a method whereby, given first-order L, a materially-adequate construction of the states of affairs posited by L can be given which meets the structural Conditions 1, $2^{\#}$, and 3. And the refinement of the earlier Condition 2 into $2^{\#}$ means there is nothing to the concern that this project is trivial, being doomed by formal results never to extend beyond the literally first-order.

7. For expository purposes it turns out easiest to tackle the task just set by way of a preliminary construction which ignores that part of Condition $2^{\#}$ which requires tight logical

equivalents to be co-descriptive, postponing till later the question of how this first attempt might be complicated to meet the full demand of Condition $2^{\#}$. This preliminary construction is based upon one devised for rather different ends by McKinsey,[7] with some differences of emphasis and detail to suit it to the present context.

Suppose given some first-order language L, formulated (let us for concreteness suppose) with $\sim$, & and $\forall$ as its logical primitives. Next, suppose that in a set-theoretical metalanguage ML of L a standard model-theory for L is developed in the fashion of the elementary logic texts, but extend that standard account slightly by requiring that a primitive predicate P^n is assigned not only an extension $\text{Ext}_M(P^n)$ relative to each model M (*i.e.* an n-place relation on D_M), but is assigned also some element $\text{Int}_M(P^n)$ as its 'intension' relative to M; and suppose that the model-theory articulates the relation between extensions and 'intensions' by containing a functor Δ, primitive or defined, such that on each model M, $\Delta(\text{Int}_M(P^n)) = \text{Ext}_M(P^n))$. Then, drawing on the resources of the contained model-theory, the preliminary construction of states of affairs can be carried forward in ML.

First, given an arbitrary model M for L, define an *atomic state of affairs* posited by L relative to M as any $n+1$-tuple $\langle \text{Int}_M(P^n), b_1 \ldots b_n \rangle$ where P^n is a primitive n-place predicate of L and each b_i is an element of D_M. Then define the set Σ_M of *states of affairs* posited by L relative to M as the smallest set Σ such that

(i) $\xi \in \Sigma$, whenever ξ is an atomic state of affairs posited by L relative to M

(ii) if $\xi \in \Sigma$, so is $\langle \sim, \xi \rangle$

and (iii) if $\Gamma \subseteq \Sigma$ then $\Gamma \in \Sigma$ (provided $|\Gamma| \geqslant |D_M| + 1$).

(In the proviso of the last condition, $|y|$ is, for any set y, the cardinal number of y. The point of the proviso is to ensure that Σ_M will contain, by the provisions to follow, enough elements to provide descripta for all L's conjunctions and quantified formulae, without allowing too many unneeded elements into the construction. And by thus cutting down the size of Σ_M to the barest minimum needed, the proviso ensures that Σ_M will

[7] In his 'New Definition'; see Bibliography.

always be a genuine *set*, given that D_M is. See more on this point below, p. 86.)

Next, we define what it is for an element ξ of Σ_M to *obtain* (according to M):

(i) if ξ is an atomic state of affairs $<\text{Int}_M(P^n)b_1 \ldots b_n>$, then ξ obtains$_M$ iff $<b_1 \ldots b_n> \in \Delta(\text{Int}_M(P^n))$.

(ii) if ξ is $<\sim, \zeta>$ for some ζ, then ξ obtains $_M$ iff ζ does not obtain$_M$

(iii) if ξ is a set of elements of Σ_M, ξ obtains$_M$ iff every member of ξ obtains$_M$.

Finally, we need a definition of the description relation which relates closed sentences of L to states of affairs in Σ_M. To get there, we first need a more general notion, that of the elements of Σ_M *assigned* under M to a (possibly open) wff A of L relative to a denumerable sequence s of members of D_M – in symbols, $\text{Ass}_M(A,s)$. We define:

(i) Suppose A is atomic, *i.e.*, A is $P^n t_1 \ldots t_n$, for some primitive predicate P^n and terms $t_1 \ldots t_n$ of L. Then $\text{Ass}_M(A,s) = <\text{Int}_M(P^n), \text{den}_M(t_1,s), \ldots \text{den}_M(t_n,s)>$ where $\text{den}_M(t_i,s)$ is the sequence-relative denotation of t_i on M, as defined in the standard underlying model-theory for L.

(ii) If A is $\sim B$ for some wff B, then $\text{Ass}_M(A,s) = <\sim, \text{Ass}_M(B,s)>$.

(iii) If A is $(B \& C)$ for some wffs, B,C then $\text{Ass}_M(A,s) = \{\text{Ass}_M(A,s), \text{Ass}_M(B,s)\}$.

(iv) If A is $(\forall v_i)B$ for some variable v_i and wff B, then $\text{Ass}_M(A,s) = \{\xi | (\exists s')(s' \text{ differs from } s \text{ in at most the } i\text{-th place} \& \xi = \text{Ass}_M(B,s'))\}$.

Then it is a simple matter to prove by induction that choice of sequence makes no difference to the element of Σ_M assigned to a *sentence* (closed wff of L on M, *i.e.* that where S is a sentence and s and s' any sequences over D_M, $\text{Ass}_M(S,s) = \text{Ass}_M(S,s')$. So the *descriptum* of a sentence S of L in M – $\text{Desc}_M(S)$ – is definable as that unique ξ in Σ_M which is $\text{Ass}_M(S,s)$ for any sequence s over D_M.

Which completes the preliminary construction. Of course its apparatus has been model-relative throughout – it has *e.g.*

defined the set Σ_M of state of affairs posited by L *relative to M*, whereas our chief interest is in the set Σ_L of states of affairs posited by L (*simpliciter*). But Σ_L is obtainable from the model relative construction given, provided the underlying model-theory developed in ML contains a designation of some model M^* as the primary or intended model for L: $\Sigma_L = \Sigma_{M^*}$. And similarly unqualified notions of descriptum and of obtaining emerge from the model relative ones: $\text{Desc}_L(S) = \text{Desc}_{M^*}(S)$, and ξ obtains$_L$ iff ξ obtains$_{M^*}$.

8.   It is obvious enough that this preliminary construction fails (as it was said it would) to assign the same descriptum to sentences which are tight logical equivalents – *e.g.* $\text{Desc}_L(\sim\sim S) = <\sim,<\sim,\text{Desc}_L(S)>> \neq \text{Desc}_L(S)$; but almost equally obvious that it satisfies the residue of Condition 2#, along with the other two structural conditions. What bears more looking at is how it fares on the score of material adequacy – of construing a sentence's descriptum recognizably as a complex whose 'constituents' are the entities relevant for the sentence's truth.

The construction's leading idea is, of course, to explicate this talk of complexity set theoretically; and at the atomic level its move is straightforwardly to identify the descriptum of an atomic sentence with a sequence of the entities relevant for its truth. The controversial feature here is the selection of 'intensions' as the truth-relevant elements corresponding to predicates, though the heart of the controversy lies less in the construction given than in the details of the model-theoretic framework within which it is undertaken. For a theorist who, rejecting Quine, thinks good sense can be made of synonymies between natural-language predicates will presumably have carried this view into his model-theory, equating its 'intensions' with genuine intensions (construed formally, say, in the style of Montague); and a construction built upon such a robust model-theory will agree with traditional views even in the strong positive thesis that sentences like 'Alfred is an aardvark' and 'Alfred is a groundhog' describe the same state of affairs, due to the synonymy of the contained predicates. Yet the construction itself is open for use too by a Quinean who, making no sense of synonymy, can yet forge a model-theory adequate to get things moving – say, a model theory which trivially identifies the 'intension' of a primitive predicate with the predicate itself.[8] A construction founded on such a spare model-theory will not, of course, join traditional views in the strong positive thesis of the co-descriptiveness of our sentences about Alfred, but will at least share with them the negative thesis that the mere co-extensiveness of the contained predicates in such sentences as 'Quine is cordate' and 'Quine is renate' is insufficient to ensure the sentences co-describe, and so may claim at the atomic level to reflect at least an austere non-intensionalist version of the tradition. On either construal of the underlying model-theory, then, the preliminary construction is reasonably regarded as embodying a materially adequate conception of states of affairs at the atomic level, so that there is no need at this point to favour one model-theory over the other; indeed, at no point in the sequel either will anything of significance depend upon the presumed viability of a more-than-Quinean model-theory.

Atomic sentences dealt with, the construction must now find a way of set-theoretically generating descripta for complex sentences out of the descripta of their parts. This it does easily and naturally enough for conjunctions and universal quantifications (in effect treating the descriptum of a conjunction as the set of the descripta of its conjuncts, and universal quantifications as possibly infinite conjunctions), but in dealing with negations it runs headlong into the traditional problem concerning 'negative facts'. This familiar headache springs in essence from a clash between the demand for material adequacy and the structural Condition 3: intuitively, the same elements are relevant for the truth of a sentence S and for its negation $\sim S$, so that by the material adequacy demand they should describe the same state of affairs; but S and $\sim S$ have opposed truth-conditions, hence by Condition 3 must have different descripta. One attractive way out of this dilemma is to argue that the elements relevant for the truth of $\sim S$ are indeed (at one level) the same as those relevant for the

---

[8] Actually, given the details of the way we have supposed the underlying model-theory to be set up, it would be better for the trivializing Quinean to make 'intensions' *pairs* of predicate-letters and models, for the sake of the smooth introduction of Δ:

$$\text{Int}_M(P^n) = <P^n, M>; \quad \Delta(<x,y>) = \text{Ext}_y(x).$$

truth of S, but that these same elements are relevant for the truth of $\sim S$ *in a different way* from that in which they are relevant for the truth of S; elevating this 'way of being truth-relevant' into an entity (the *negative mode*), we may then conclude that (at a deeper level) there is after all one entity relevant for the truth of $\sim S$ over and above those relevant for the truth of S, and accordingly require that the descriptum of $\sim S$ be a complex containing the descriptum of S plus one extra entity – the negative mode. And this plausible path is just the one our initial construction takes, adding one extra step – that of identifying that mysterious entity, the negative mode, with the negation sign itself. If the last step is found implausible, the construction is easily modified by the identification of the negative mode with any other more familiar thing, or by taking it as an undefined primitive; in any case, it seems to handle a traditional problem in as good a way as any.

9.   We turn now to the problem of modifying this preliminary construction so as to obtain another which, by assigning the same descriptum to any two sentences which are tight logical equivalents, meets Condition $2^{\#}$ in its full strength. As a prelude to this, consider first the problem of extending the construction by defining over the states of affairs in Σ_L a relation $\doteqdot$ of *L-relative equivalence*, which provably holds between the descripta of any two sentences of L which are tight logical equivalents – the problem, in other words, of defining $\doteqdot$ over Σ_L in such a way as to permit proof of the

> *Equivalence Theorem.* If S and S' are tight logical equivalents, then $\mathrm{Desc}_L(S) \doteqdot \mathrm{Desc}_L(S')$.[9]

I owe the approach I shall adopt to this preliminary problem to Michael Dummett, who suggested it as an improvement on halting steps I had taken in another direction. Let Σ_L^{AT} be the set of *atomic* states of affairs in L, let an *atomic set-up* for L be any subset of Σ_L^{AT}, and let the *actual* atomic set-up for L be that

---

[9] Alternatively, we could consider the more general problem of defining $\doteqdot$ over Σ_M, for M an arbitrary model, in such a way as to ensure provability of the Equivalence Theorem in a generalized form. And indeed, the method to be sketched solves the more general problem too, since nowhere depending on assumed special features of L's primary model M^*; I state the problem

atomic set-up whose elements are precisely the atomic states of affairs in Σ_L which according to L obtain. Then it is possible to associate each state of affairs ξ, atomic or complex, in Σ_L, with an *L-range*; a set of atomic set-ups for L such that ξ obtains according to L just in case L's actual atomic set-up is an element of ξ's L-range. Formally, we define:

(i) If ξ is atomic, then $\text{Range}_L(\xi) = \{\Gamma | \xi \in \Gamma \,\&\, \Gamma \subseteq \Sigma_L^{AT}\}$

(ii) If ξ is $<\sim,\zeta>$ for some ζ, then
$\text{Range}_L(\xi) = \mathscr{P}\,\Sigma_L^{AT} - \text{Range}_L(\zeta)$

(iii) If ξ is a set of elements of Σ_L, then
$\text{Range}_L(\xi) = \bigcap_{\zeta \in \xi} \text{Range}_L(\zeta)$.

And now, intuitively, we ought to be able to show that the state of affairs ξ a tight logical truth describes has as its L-range the totality of atomic set-ups for L – for otherwise, it seems, ξ would fail to obtain if the actual atomic set-up for L happened to fall outside ξ's L-range; yet presumably, as the descriptum of a tight logical truth ξ could never fail to obtain. That is, intuition leads us to expect to be able to establish the

Range Lemma. If S is a tight logical truth, then
$\text{Range}_L(\text{Desc}_L(S)) = \mathscr{P}\,\Sigma_L^{AT}$

and this is indeed forthcoming quite formally, as is demonstrated in detail in this chapter's Postscript. Further, from this result we can move to a

Corollary. If S and S' are tight logical equivalents then
$\text{Range}_L(\text{Desc}_L(S)) = \text{Range}_L(\text{Desc}_L(S'))$

(where I relegate the details of the move once more to the Postscript). And from the Corollary it follows that we will ensure provability of the key Equivalence Theorem if we define

Definition $\overset{.}{\le}$. Where ξ,ζ are elements of Σ_L,
$\xi \overset{.}{\le} \zeta \leftrightarrow \text{Range}_L(\xi) = \text{Range}_L(\zeta)$.

(For suppose S, S' tight logical equivalents; then $\text{Range}_L(\text{Desc}_L(S)) = \text{Range}_L(\text{Desc}_L(S'))$, by the Corollary; so $\text{Desc}_L(S) \overset{.}{\le} \text{Desc}_L(S')$, by the definition of $\overset{.}{\le}$.)

---

and its solution in the current more specific terms merely to emphasize the fact that our interest from now on will be exclusively in the elements of Σ_L and their properties, the sets Σ_M for arbitrary M having entered the picture at all solely as a handy way of getting at the entities of primary interest.

With $\doteqdot$ defined, it is a simple matter to transmute the earlier preliminary construction into one meeting all the earlier structural conditions, including Condition 2# in its full strength: just redefine the states of affairs posited by L as equivalence classes over Σ_L under $\doteqdot$, take the descriptum of a sentence as being now the equivalence-class to which its old descriptum belongs, and construe a new state of affairs as obtaining iff all its elements obtain in the old sense.[10] Then the proofs that Conditions 1 and 3 are met is trivial, and given the Range Lemma it is easily shown that if sentences S and S' are tightly chainwise connected then $\mathrm{Desc}_L(S) \doteqdot \mathrm{Desc}_L(S')$, whence the new construction must meet Condition 2# as well. And further, it seems the new construction must fare at least as well on the score of material adequacy as did its predecessor, since it can simply be ruled that in the sense of constituent appropriate to the new construction, the 'constituents' of S's new complex descriptum are to be counted the same as those embedded in the old-style descriptum which figures as an element of the new one. But, beyond the mere desire to show that it is possible to preserve the strict letter of the conditions we earlier imposed, there is little point in complicating the old construction along these lines; for working purposes we surely do better to stick with the simpler conception of states of affairs as elements of Σ_L, and to rest content with speaking of states of affairs as merely equivalent in some cases where a more orthodox theory would talk rather of identity. So that is the course I shall take, noting however that no more than cumbrous inelegance is the price to be paid for stricter conformity with my original conditions and traditional views.

10.   A couple of final points about this construction. A point just made has been that the theory proposed meets (its version of) Condition 2#, by assigning equivalent descripta to sentences which are tightly chainwise connected. But it is obvious that this result can be strengthened: equivalent

---

[10] Another way to turn the trick might seem to be to take $\mathscr{P}\,\Sigma_L^{\wedge\mathrm{T}}$ as the set of states of affairs L posits, and then to identify S's descriptum with the L-range of $\mathrm{Desc}_L(S)$. But this suggestion fares poorly on the score of material adequacy – it would, for example, count the descriptum of $\sim S$ as having no constituents at all in common with the descriptum of S itself.

descripta are also assigned to sentences linked by an *extended* tight sentence chain, *i.e.* sentences linked by a sentence-sequence $S_1 \ldots S_n$ satisfying our earlier requirements for tight chainwise connectedness but with the additional proviso that links may also be forged by substitution of primitive predicates with the same 'intension' (S_{i+1} may be $S_i(Q^n//P^n)$ if $\text{Int}_L(P^n) = \text{Int}_L(Q^n)$). It will be recalled that, when Condition 2 was originally introduced, we toyed with the possibility of stating it in terms of a stronger notion of chainwise connexion which would permit connexion to involve the substitution of *synonymous* primitive predicates, but shrank from imposing it outright to avoid committing our construction *ab initio* to a full-blooded intensionalism. The significance of what has just been observed is that if, nevertheless, the underlying model-theory should happen to embody a notion of 'intension' strong enough for predicates it reckons cointensive to be reckoned genuinely synonymous, the construction given will meet the strong condition we earlier refused to require outright.

The notion of an extended tight sentence-chain can be put to use too to make a second point. It will be noticed that none of the structural conditions imposed hitherto have laid down a *necessary* condition for two sentences being co-descriptive, and in this omission they do I think faithfully reflect a tradition which has no clear consensus on the matter. Nevertheless, it transpires that the particular construction here advocated does permit precise statement of an analogous necessary condition for two sentences describing equivalent states of affairs, at least for quantifier-free sentences. For so far as such sentences go the converse of the last point also holds; *i.e.* we can establish a

> *Linking Theorem.* If S and S' are quantifier-free and $\text{Desc}_L(S) \not\approx \text{Desc}_L(S')$, then S and S' are linked by an extended tight sentence-chain.

(Proof in the Postscript.) Here, however, the restriction to the quantifier-free is essential, since if the domain of L's intended model is finite our construction allows conjunctions and universal quantifications to describe equivalent states of affairs despite the lack of a connecting sentence-chain; in allowing which possibility, it follows one strand (the anti-Russellian, Ramseyan one) of the tradition it is out to explicate.

Postscript to Chapter 2

Proofs of Formal Results

(A) Proof of the Range Lemma

Contraposing the Lemma and recalling that the tight logical truths are prcisely those true in all (standard) models of L, it will suffice to prove

[I] If $\text{Range}_L(\text{Desc}_L(S)) \neq \mathscr{P} \Sigma_L^{\text{AT}}$, then there is a model M for L s.t. S is false on M.

For each element Γ of $\mathscr{P} \Sigma_L^{\text{AT}}$ and wff A of L, let M be a model *induced by* Γ and A iff

(i) $D_M = D_{M^*}$ (where M^* is the primary, designated model)

(ii) for each P^n, $<b_1 \ldots b_n> \in \text{Ext}_M(P^n)$ iff $<\text{Int}_{M^*}(P^n) b_1 \ldots b_n> \in \Gamma$

and (iii) for each term t in A and sequence s,
$\text{den}_M(t, s) = \text{den}_{M^*}(t, s)$.

Then – *cf.* Remark below – for each Γ and A there is a model M induced by Γ and A. And by induction on the complexity of A, we establish

Lemma 1. If M is induced by Γ and A, then s satisfies A on M iff $\Gamma \in \text{Range}_L(\text{Ass}_{M^*}(A, s))$.

[I] follows: if $\text{Range}_L(\text{Desc}_L(S)) \neq \mathscr{P}\Sigma_L^{\text{AT}}$, then there is some Γ in $\mathscr{P}\Sigma_L^{\text{AT}}$ which is not a member of $\text{Range}_L(\text{Desc}_L(S))$, whence by Lemma 1 S is false on some model M induced by Γ and S.

Remark. Where L is, as supposed, straightforwardly first-order, there is obviously for each Γ and A a model M meeting conditions (i)–(iii), in particular, condition (iii) is met just by having M make the same assignments to functors and individual constants as does M^*. But if L is extended by adding a description operator, (iii) is harder to meet. It *can* be met just by making finitely many outright stipulations that the desired instances of (iii) are true, but then the resulting induced model M may treat the description-operator non-standardly. That, however, does not invalidate the proof of the Range Lemma even when applied to such an extended language, since the *tight* logical truths must be true even on models non-standard in their treatment of the description operator.

(B) Proof of Corollary

Suppose S and S' tight logical equivalents; then (i) $S \to S'$ is a tight logical truth, and (ii) so is $S' \to S$. From (i) and the Range Lemma,

$$\text{Range}_L(\text{Desc}_L(S \to S')) = \mathscr{P}\Sigma_L^{\text{AT}}$$

Hence

$$\mathscr{P}\Sigma_L^{\text{AT}} = (\mathscr{P}\Sigma_L^{\text{AT}} - \text{Range}_L(\text{Desc}_L(S))) \cup$$
$$\text{Range}_L(\text{Desc}_L(S'))$$

(the right hand side being another way of specifying $\text{Range}_L(\text{Desc}_L(S \to S'))$, as calculated by the formal definitions of range and descriptum once $\to$ is cashed out in terms of $\sim$ and &). But in general, if $a = (a - b) \cup c$, then $b \subseteq c$; so $\text{Range}_L(\text{Desc}_L(S)) \subseteq \text{Range}_L(\text{Desc}_L(S'))$. Similarly from (ii) $\text{Range}_L(\text{Desc}_L(S') \subseteq \text{Range}_L(\text{Desc}_L(S))$. Combine the two for the result.

(C) Proof of the Linking Theorem

For each P^n, let $\overline{P^n}$ be some arbitrarily selected cointensive predicate letter; for each closed term t let $\bar{t}$ be an arbitrarily selected coreferential closed term; and let the *normalization* $N(S)$ of S be the result of replacing each P^n and closed term t in S by $\overline{P^n}$ and $\bar{t}$. Then evidently, for any S, S and $N(S)$ are linked by an extended tight sentence-chain of L; so to prove the theorem it is enough to establish

> *Lemma 2.* If S and S' are quantifier-free and $\mathrm{Desc}_L(S) \doteqdot \mathrm{Desc}_L(S')$, then $N(S)$ and $N(S')$ are tight logical equivalents.

Call a sentence S *normal* iff $S = N(S)$; and let a *normal valuation* for L be an assignment of truth-values to normal quantifier-free wffs of L which respects the usual rules for $\sim$ and $\&$ (so that a normal quantifier-free sentence is a tight logical truth iff it is assigned T by every normal valuation). Further, let v be the normal valuation *induced by* an element Γ of $\mathscr{P}\Sigma_L^{\mathrm{AT}}$ just in case, for each normal atomic sentence S of L, $v(S) = \mathrm{T}$ iff $\mathrm{Desc}_L(S) \in \Gamma$. Then by induction on the complexity of S, we can establish

> *Lemma 3.* If S is a normal quantifier-free sentence, then the normal valuations which assign T to S are precisely those induced by elements of $\mathrm{Range}_L(\mathrm{Desc}_L(S))$.

> *Lemma 4.* For any sentence S, $\mathrm{Desc}_L(S) = \mathrm{Desc}_L(N(S))$.

Lemma 2 follows. For suppose its hypothesis; then by Lemma 4, $\mathrm{Desc}_L(N)S)) \doteqdot \mathrm{Desc}_L(N(S'))$; so by Lemma 3 precisely the same normal valuations assign T to $N(S)$ as to $N(S')$, *i.e.* the two are tight logical equivalents.

3

Tenses and Verbs

1. I want to construe events as a species of states of affairs, and, the last chapter having concerned itself with the nature of the containing genus, it is time to consider the differentiae of the contained species. The Aristotelian ring of this way of putting things is, as it happens, appropriate, since I want to argue that it is by way of a classification of verbs The Philosopher devised that events are to be singled out from states of affairs generally. And it will be the business of this chapter to explicate the classification, that of the next to put it to use to show how events are distinguished.

2. Aristotle's taxonomy of verbs proceeds by way of properties they exhibit in their continuous tenses. Any explication of it therefore requires a prior account of the nature of these tenses, and that in turn presupposes an underlying framework judged adequate to handle the less complex non-continuous tenses. Our first task must accordingly be that of choosing a suitable underlying framework – *i.e.* of selecting a formalism apt to provide base structures capable of reflecting at least the simplest tense features of surface English (features ignored, along with all other indexical characteristics, in anything yet said about base structures); with an eye to later complication which will be capable of accommodating the more sophisticated continuous versions of the tenses as well.

There are philosophers who, faced with any demand for

formal elucidation of temporal locutions, reach at once for heavy Quinean artillery, and propose the use of a paraphrasing symbolism whose variables range, not over the familiar three-dimensional items of commonsense, but rather over unchanging four-dimensional objects which extend through time as well as space. But whatever the merits of this manoeuvre as a proposal for a canonical *deviation* from ordinary English for the purposes of science or metaphysics, it will be clear that the paraphrases it offers are unsuited, by the lights of the opening sections of Chapter One, for construal as base structures for English sentences. For the radical conceptual reorientation these paraphrases involve renders them inappropriate to figure as the foundation of a theory of sense whose aim is to assign to uttered sentences those contents of associated speech-acts which are regularly and systematically assigned by everyday English-speakers who rest content with the concepts their language hands them.

Fortunately, contemporary wisdom provides a choice of two less radical ways for rendering the subtleties of tense into formalism. One method is to augment first-order apparatus by adding *tense-operators*: indexical sentential operators used to generate tensed renditions out of tenseless first-order formulae. The other way – Frege's – is to require that ostensibly n-place predicates of surface English capable of being tensed be represented in the formalism by $n + 1$-place predicates, the extra argument-place being reserved for occupancy by a singular-term for a *time*; tense is then to be accommodated by means of a system of terms (some of them indexical) denoting times, along with predicates expressive of properties and relations of the times thus invoked.

Although most attention in recent years has concentrated on the first of these alternatives, in the present context Frege's strategy has a number of advantages. To begin with, the whole point of our current concern with tense is ultimately to explicate an Aristotelian classification of *verbs*; so it looks more appealing to begin with an account which in Frege's fashion treats tense as a feature of *predicates* underlying verbs rather than as a characteristic attaching to whole *sentences* (as the competing operator strategy makes it appear). Again, Frege's proposal involves minimal distortion of the working picture, adopted in abstraction from indexical considerations back in Chapter One's second section, of the base structures of English as straightforwardly first-order. For it complicates first-order devices merely by adding indexical singular terms, and some such complication was surely going to be required once indexicality was given full attention – just to accommodate the brute indexicality of 'That is red', without worrying about its more subtle manifestation in tense. And further, the extensions to Tarskian methods required to yield, for a first-order symbolism thus supplemented, an austerely-adequate theory of truth apt to function as a theory of sense, have been well researched by writers such as Burge and Weinstein;[1] whereas by comparison the austere truth-theory (as distinct from the model-theory) of the operator approach is uncharted water.[2]

Settling accordingly on a Fregean approach, let us be more precise about the formal resources we need to assume available in the regimenting symbolism in order to implement it. First, of course, we need indexical temporal terms – 'now', at least, and perhaps also 'then'. Further, variables of the base formalism must be construed as ranging over a domain embracing *times*; and apparently times of two sorts will need to be acknowledged, since any sophisticated account of temporal locutions must appeal to indivisible temporal *moments*, whilst at the same time many typical temporal singular terms of English (*e.g.* 'Thursday afternoon') evidently refer not to moments but to longer temporal *periods*. So it is natural to think of the base symbolism as containing predicates 'Mom(t)' ('t is a moment') and 'Per(t)' ('t is a period') to mark the bifurcation of its

---

[1] See the works by these authors in the Bibliography. My own views on the matter are in my paper 'Truth Theory'. (In fact, in that paper I argue that indexical 'terms' are really best treated as a species of quantifier; whereas in the present work I use a symbolism apparently at odds with this view. I maintain nevertheless that the incompatibility is superficial, and that there is no problem in translating systematically from the formalism of the present work into that of the paper, which remains my official view on matters indexical.)

[2] The only work I know of on this matter was in an early draft of a paper by Gareth Evans due to appear in the Davidson *Festschrift* referred to in the Bibliography with respect to Wiggins' paper; but not having seen the final version I am not sure how much emphasis will ultimately be placed there on the topic.

temporal domain. Further, the symbolism will need predicates to express *relations* between times: I write '$t < t'$' to mean 't is *earlier than t'*', '$t \sqsubset t'$' to mean 't *falls properly (wholly) within t'*', and '$t \sqsubseteq t'$' to mean 't *falls within t'*' (*i.e. t* either falls properly within t', or else is the whole of t'). (Evidently, the temporal notions just invoked and the theory of the nature of times they presuppose call out for systematic articulation; moreover, for an articulation which shuns the natural use of set-theory, lest the formalism we deploy be suspected of commitment to powerful conceptual resources rendering it unsuitable for the framing of *base* structures. In the Postscript to this chapter, I proffer accordingly an axiomatic theory of times construed as densely and continuously ordered, and taking as primitive just the relations of identity and temporal precedence. The account there developed constitutes my official account of the temporal notions to which this chapter will appeal; but an intuitive construal will suffice to follow my argument.)

In addition to these specifically temporal resources, our Fregean base symbolism must also of course contain the time-relativized predicates which are to do the crucial work in the representation of tense. Ultimately, the significance of this relativization must be taken as primitive, and clarified by the use to which the relativized predicates are put; but one source of possible future confusion can be cut off at once. For it is natural to think of the time to which a predicate is relativized as giving the time *at which* the predicate is said to be instantiated, and so to give a formula like

(1) Hirsute (Esau, t)

the sense of the English

(1′) Esau is hirsute at t.

But the proprieties of English render this construal unattractive in the present context. For in English the preposition 'at' is happily followed only by a singular-term referring to a temporal *moment*; whereas, as the sequel will reveal, it is necessary sometimes to regard the temporal argument-place of a Fregean predicate as occupied by a singular term for a longer temporal *period*. So I recommend for (1) in place of (1′) the construal

(1″) *t* is a time of Esau's being hirsute

which, just because it is less-than-idiomatic English, gives a reading of the symbolism less likely to carry unwanted overtones than its predecessor.

With the resources adumbrated presumed present in the symbolism of the base, it is now child's play to manipulate them to obtain Fregean base paraphrases for English sentences in the simple tenses. For the *simple present* of

(2) Esau is hirsute

(verb-tensed) becomes

(2i) Hirsute (Esau,now)

whilst the *simple past* and *simple future* exemplified respectively in

(3) Esau was hirsute
(3) Esau will be hirsute

go over dually as

(3i) $(\exists t)(t < \text{now } \& \text{ Hirsute(Esau, } t))$
and (4i) $(\exists t)(\text{now } < t \& \text{ Hirsute(Esau, } t))$.

3. It is less clear how the perfect tenses are to be accommodated. The obvious move on the *present* perfect, exemplified in

(5) Esau has been hirsute

is to assign to it the base paraphrase (3i); but this obvious ploy, though I believe it to be correct, generates a puzzle. For in assigning to the perfect-tensed (5) the same base paraphrases as the simple-tensed (3), we commit ourselves to treating the two sentences as semantically equivalent; yet some differences between the two must be accounted for, since they are non-interchangeable in standard English speech.

Seeking a solution to the problem, we could do worse than begin by invoking the apparatus developed by Reichenbach in his celebrated discussion of tense.[3] Reichenbach distinguishes

[3] See his *Elements*, section 5.1.

three times associated with each utterance of a tensed sentence, *viz.*

(i) the *point of speech*, *i.e.* the time at which the utterance is made,

(ii) the *point of the event*, *i.e.* the time at which the speaker asserts the event (or state) described in the sentence to occur (or obtain),

(iii) the *point of reference*, *i.e.* the temporal standpoint from which the speaker invites his audience to consider the occurrence of the event (or the obtaining of the state).

In uttering a sentence cast in a simple tense, Reichenbach goes on to claim, a speaker's reference-point is to be taken as identical with the point of the event, which in turn he asserts to be simultaneous with, prior to, or subsequent upon the point of speech according as his utterance is in the present, past, or future simple tense. A systematic account of the relationship between the perfect and simple tenses then emerges: the temporal points associated with an utterance of a perfect-tensed sentence are to be supposed related as far as possible in the same way as they are in an utterance of a sentence in the corresponding simple tense, subject to the overriding requirement that the point of reference is to be *later* than the point of the event. The relations indicated between the temporal points associated with utterances of sentences in simple and perfect tenses may therefore be represented under obvious diagrammatic conventions as shown opposite (where the points marked 'S', 'E', and 'R' represent respectively the points of speech, event, and reference).

The structure Reichenbach reveals shows that the simple past of (3) and the present perfect of (5) differ only in denominating one of the other two associated temporal points as the point of reference. To treat utterances of the two sentences as equivalent semantically, as I have suggested we should by according both the same base paraphrase (3i), accordingly amounts to saying that this denomination makes no difference to truth-conditions (nor to the content the utterances convey, since the contemplated truth-theory is to function as a theory of sense). And that looks right – for in

	Simple	Perfect
Present	S, R, E	E S, R
Past	E, R S	E R S
Future	S E,R	S E R

assertively uttering either (3) or (5), a speaker surely asserts the same thing, namely that Esau was hirsute at some earlier time. Still, we can account for the differences between the two tenses in terms of *pragmatics*, that component of total linguistic theory which seeks to elucidate the principles governing features of use which remain unaccounted for by the theory of sense. For we can say that in choosing the simple-tensed forms of words (3) a speaker uses a conventional device to direct the attention of his audience to the earlier time of event as his reference-point, whilst in selecting the perfect-tensed (5) it is rather to the present time of utterance that attention is drawn.

In the case of the past and future perfect tenses, on the other hand, the reference-point of an utterance is distinct from either of the other two Reichenbachian points, and it seems natural to say that explicit reference to this further time is part of the literal content of an assertion the utterance conveys. Any such reference moreover is presumably achieved by a further act of temporal demonstration. So for the *past* perfect of

    (6) Esau had been hirsute

and the *future* perfect of

    (7) Esau will have been hirsute

I suggest accordingly the Fregean paraphrases

(6i) $(\exists t)(t < $ then & then $<$ now & Hirsute (Esau, t))
and (7i) $(\exists t)($ now $< t$ & $t <$ then & Hirsute (Esau, t))

where, on each occasion of utterance, the demonstrative 'then' serves to indicate the reference-point of the speaker.

4. The stage is now set for the main business of this chapter: an account of the continuous tenses, and of Aristotle's classification of verbs of natural languages in terms of properties of their continuous tenses. Aristotle's classification[4] is a trichotomy, which would distinguish amongst the verb-phrases of English:
(a) S('state')-verbs, *e.g.* 'is hirsute', 'is red', 'is soluble', 'is taller than (Caesar)', 'loves (Beatrice)', 'understands (Godel's proof)'. The distinguishing characteristic of S-verbs is that they do not occur in genuine continuous tenses in standard English speech.
(b) E('*energeia*')-verbs, *e.g.* 'chuckles', 'talks', 'blushes', 'moves', 'strokes (the dog)', 'ponders'. E-verbs are distinguished by the fact that, for E-verbs V, the present continuous 'x is V-ing' entails the perfect 'x has V-ed'.
(c) K('*kinesis*')-verbs, *e.g.* 'stabs (Caesar)', 'discovers (America)', 'builds (the house)', 'polishes (the boot)', 'grows up'. K-verbs are distinguished by possessing a *contrary* property to that characteristic of E-verbs, a fact commonly expressed by saying that for K-verbs, 'x is V-ing' entails 'x has not V-ed'; though it is clear that this slogan cannot be taken as a precise expression of the property in question. For the account of the present perfect given in the last section permits distinction of two senses in which the phrase 'x has not V-ed' may be taken, depending on the scope of the negation; that is, we may construe the phrase as meaning (roughly) either

(i) $\sim(\exists t)(t < $ now & t is a time of x's V-ing)
or (ii) $(\exists t)(t < $ now & $\sim(t$ is a time of x's V-ing)).

And yet under neither of these construals does the common slogan accurately express a property which can be taken as

----

[4] See *e.g. Metaphysics* Θ 6 (1048 b 18–35); *Nicomachean Ethics* X 4.

definitive of K-verbs. 'Brutus is stabbing Caesar' does not entail 'Brutus has not stabbed Caesar' in sense (i) of the latter expression, since the current stabbing may be Brutus' second for the morning. And for E-verbs *as well as* K-verbs it is true that '*x* is V-ing' entails '*x* has not V-ed' in sense (ii). No time need be wasted, however, in a search for refinements of vernacular formulations avoiding these difficulties, provided a formal account of the properties of E-verbs underlying their characteristic entailments can be found. For then we may hope a candidate for a contrary property to be attributed to K-verbs will emerge, and the common slogan, despite its imperfections, should be suggestive enough to permit evaluation of any such candidate.

To approach the account I want to give of these distinctions and the continuous tenses giving rise to them, consider the case of Rod, a hirsute barman, who pulls a pint, taking all the time in some period P to do so, and chuckles the while. Then it is reasonable to say, of any moment m within P, that m is a time of Rod's being hirsute; indeed, P counts as a time of Rod's being hirsute, it seems, just because each moment m within P is such a time. On the other hand, although at each moment m within P it is true to say that Rod *is chuckling* and *is pulling a pint*, it is plausible to hold that no moment within P can be a time *of* Rod's chuckling or of his pulling a pint; for both pulling pints and chuckling take time in a way in which being hirsute does not. These remarks suggest that the continuous tenses may be construed as functioning so as to mark the presence of a time t (typically a moment) which, *though not itself a time of application of the tensed verb*, occurs within a more inclusive time which *is* a period of the verb's application. This construal explains both why continuous tensings of K- and E-verbs can be true at times which are not themselves times of application of the verb, and also why S-verbs should lack continuous tenses – for every time within a period of application of such a verb itself being a time of its application, there is no place for tenses designed to register the existence of times of non-application of the verb within broader periods of its application.

These informal views are elucidated by the following symbolism. I assume that verb-phrases in each of the categories of S-, K-, and E-verbs will be represented in the base by use of a predicate constant in the corresponding category, to be defined below as the theory is developed. Where P_j^n is the j-th n-place predicate constant of the base formalism, let V_j^n be the result of filling its first $n - 1$ argument places by distinct variables (say, the first $n - 1$ variables in some specified standard ordering).[5] The formal upshot of the above remarks on S-verbs is then that P_j^n should count as an S-predicate iff it meets

> *Postulate 1*　　$\mathrm{Per}(t) \rightarrow (V_j^n t \leftrightarrow (\forall t')(\mathrm{Mom}(t') \ \&$
> $t' \sqsubset t . \rightarrow . V_j^n t'))$

so that, for example the predicate 'Hirsute' is an S-predicate on the assumption that it fits

> *Postulate 1a*　　$\mathrm{Per}(t) \rightarrow (\mathrm{Hirsute}(x,t) \leftrightarrow (\forall t')(\mathrm{Mom}(t') \ \&$
> $t' \sqsubset t . \rightarrow . \mathrm{Hirsute}(x,t')))$.

Again, the thesis that mere moments do not suffice as times of application for E- and K-verbs issues in the requirement that where P_j^n is an E- or K-predicate, it should meet

> *Postulate 2*　　$V_j^n t \rightarrow \mathrm{Per}(t)$

so that, *e.g.*, the E-predicate 'Chuckle' and the K-predicate 'Stab' will respectively fit

> *Postulate 2a*　　$\mathrm{Chuckle}(x,t) \rightarrow \mathrm{Per}(t)$
> *Postulate 2b*　　$\mathrm{Stab}(x,y,t) \rightarrow \mathrm{Per}(t)$.

Finally, the analysis of the continuous tenses can be expressed in intuitive symbolism by means of the schema

> *Cont*　　P_j^n-ing $x_1 \ldots x_{n-1} t \leftrightarrow \sim V_j^n t \ \& \ (\exists t')(t \sqsubset t') \ \& \ V_j^n t')$.

(The left-hand side may be read here in quasi-English as 'x_1 is P_j^n-ing $x_2 \ldots x_{n-1}$ at t'.') Combining this account of the continuous with the paraphrases of the last section, therefore, we will assign respectively to

　(8)　Brutus is stabbing Caesar
　(9)　Brutus was stabbing Caesar
　(10) Brutus will be stabbing Caesar

---

[5] In using this convention in the sequel, I assume that 'x' and 'y' are the first two variables in this standard ordering (and also that the parentheses I habitually insert around terms following predicates in atomic formulae are no strict requirement for well-formedness in the symbolism, but just a convenient embellishment to aid construal).

the base paraphrases:

(8i) $\sim$Stab(Brutus,Caesar,now) & $(\exists t')$ (now $\sqsubseteq t'$ & Stab(Brutus,Caesar,t'))

(9i) $(\exists t)(t < $ now & $\sim$Stab(Brutus,Caesar,t)) & $(\exists t')(t \sqsubseteq t'$ & Stab(Brutus,Caesar,t')))

(10i) $(\exists t)$ (now $< t$ & $\sim$Stab(Brutus,Caesar,t)) & $(\exists t')(t \sqsubseteq t')$ & Stab(Brutus,Caesar,t')))

The informal explanation given for the failure of S-verbs to occur in the continuous tenses is now reflected in the formalism by the fact that a sentence like

(11) Esau is being hirsute

receiving the base paraphrase

(11i) $\sim$Hirsute(Esau,now) & $(\exists t')$ (now $\sqsubseteq t'$ & Hirsute(Esau,t'))

is trivially false in virtue of Postulate 1a, which entails by the logic of times that for any x, t and t',

$t \sqsubseteq t'$ & Hirsute$(x,t') \rightarrow$ Hirsute(x,t).

5. Postulate 2 expresses a feature common to both K- and E-verbs, and we now turn to the problem of describing the further properties of E-verbs needed to account for their characteristic entailment. Let us say that a temporal period t is *open-fronted* $(OF(t))$ iff it contains within it no earliest moment; and dually, that a period t is *open-ended* $(OE(t))$ iff it contains within it no latest moment. Then the following two further assumptions need to be made to accommodate the peculiarities of E-verbs: (a) that every period of application of an E-predicate falls within (though not necessarily properly within) an open-fronted temporal period which is itself a period of its application; and
(b) that every *period* falling within a period of application of an E-predicate is itself a period of its application.

The first of these assumptions is a weakened version of a thesis argued for by Aristotle (*Physics* 236a, 7–28), *viz.* (in effect) that *all* periods of application of *both* E-predicates and K-predicates are open-fronted. Aristotle's arguments, however, hardly establish the point; his best one proceeds from the premise of the existence of a latest moment within any period immediately preceding a period of application of a K- or E-predicate and then argues from the density of the moments to the open-frontedness of that period itself, but no reason is given for accepting the crucial premise. The weaker assumption (a) is, however, all that is needed here, and I see no bar to accepting it even without subsidiary argument if it is needed to accommodate the data. (In particular, I do not think it is refuted empirically by examples of the sort advanced in discussion by Christopher Peacocke, whose alarm-clock rings at the laudable hour of 7a.m. – for, though 'ring' (as said of alarm-clocks) is certainly an E-verb, there is no reason to classify 7a.m. as the first moment of the period of the alarm-clock's ringing, rather than as the lower bound of that period, hence possibly as the last moment of the preceding period.)

The second of my assumptions is open to more serious objection, as the next section will reveal; but for the moment let it be accepted in the same spirit, as a working hypothesis to accommodate the data. Combining both assumptions with Postulate 2, we are left with the view that E-predicates P_j^n will be those meeting

Postulate 3 $V_j^n t \rightarrow \text{Per}(t)$ & $(\exists t')(\text{OF}(t')$ & $t \sqsubseteq t'$ &
$V_j^n t')$ & $(\forall t'')(t'' \sqsubset t$ & $\text{Per}(t'') \rightarrow V_j^n t'')$

so that, *e.g.*, the E-predicate 'Fall' will operate under

Postulate 3a $\text{Fall}(x,t) \rightarrow \text{Per}(t)$ & $(\exists t')(\text{OF}(t')$ &
$t \sqsubseteq t'$ & $\text{Fall}(x,t'))$ & $(\forall t'')(t'' \sqsubset t$ &
$\text{Per}(t'') \rightarrow \text{Fall}(x,t''))$.

Granted the further plausible supposition that the demonstrative 'now' always serves to indicate a *moment* (designating *e.g.* on each occasion of its use the least upper bound of the time taken for its utterance), this postulate combines with our analyses of the tenses and intuitive properties of times to explain the characteristic entailment of E-verbs. For suppose *e.g.* that x is falling, *i.e.* by *Cont* that there is a t such that now $\sqsubset t$ and $\text{Fall}(x,t)$. By Postulate 3a, t is open-fronted; from this and the density of moments there are accordingly moments m and m' within t such that $m < m' <$ now. So there is a period t'

stretching from m to m' which is within t and earlier than now; by the former property and Postulate 3a, Fall(x,t'); hence by our account of the simple perfect, x has fallen. Since moreover this informal reasoning can be reconstructed as a formal deduction within the theory of the Postscript, we have thus apparently arrived at a rigorous account of the idiosyncrasies of E-verbs.

6. Further, this account of E-verbs seems to yield, as was hoped, a plausible candidate explicating that contrary property of K-verbs which is suggestively if imprecisely captured in the standard slogan that for such verbs V, 'x is V-ing' entails 'x has not V-ed'. For it appears that such a candidate emerges if we assume that K-predicates possess a property contrary to that supposed above as assumption (b) to hold good of E-verbs – thus that for any K-predicate, *no* period within a period of its application should itself be such a period. Combining this assumption with Postulate 2, the K-predicates P_j^n therefore emerge as those meeting

Postulate 4 $\quad V_j^n \to \text{Per}(t)$ & $(\forall t')(t' \sqsubset t \to \sim V_j^n t')$

so that the predicate 'Stab', for example, will fit

Postulate 4a $\quad \text{Stab}(x,y,t) \to \text{Per}(t)$ &
$\qquad\qquad (\forall t')(t' \sqsubset t \to \sim\text{Stab}(x,y,t'))$.

On this view, accordingly, 'x is stabbing y' will entail a statement which we may read as 'x has not yet stabbed y during *this* period of his stabbing' – which, though hardly vernacular, is reasonably construed as the truth which the common slogan tries to capture.

We have now arrived at an account of Aristotle's taxonomy of verbs: taking *Cont* as giving the analysis of the continuous tenses, S-verbs are those regimented by predicates satisfying Postulate 1, whilst the predicates underlying K- and E-verbs satisfy Postulate 2; and E-verbs differ from K-verbs inasmuch as the predicates underlying the former meet Postulate 3, while those underpinning the latter conform rather to the contrary Postulate 4. Call this the 'Preliminary Account'. As my terminology suggests, I think it benefits from extension and revision. But before turning to these matters, let me devote a section to turning an objection which arises even to the preliminary version.

7. This objection arises from the fact that the analysis of continuity enshrined in *Cont* has as a consequence that no action can ever be *being* performed unless, eventually, it counts as *having been* performed; for '*x* was V-ing', by *Cont*, entails that some time is a time of *x*'s V-ing. This is hardly an exceptionable consequence when V is an E-verb, E-verbs being what they are. But when V is a K-verb, it looks more troublesome. For at the time of the Porlock person's untimely arrival, surely Coleridge was writing 'Kubla Khan'; but 'Kubla Khan' (the projected epic, rather than the fragment we know by the same name) was never written. And Caesar was walking to (not just towards) the Senate house when the conspirators ensured he never got there.

One writer who has taken this puzzle very seriously – seriously enough, indeed, to single it out for baptism, dubbing it the 'imperfective paradox' – is David Dowty.[6] Dowty began by offering an analysis of the continuous essentially the same as that I have advocated, differing only in omitting that first conjunct of the analysans which I supplied to secure the result that continuous tensings of S-verbs should turn out literally false. So Dowty's initial stab[7] at dealing with the continuous is

$$Cont* P_j^n\text{-ing } x_1 \ldots x_{n-1} \; t \leftrightarrow (\exists t')(t \sqsubset t' \;\&\; V_j^n t')$$

which gives rise to the imperfective paradox every bit as much as my own slightly stronger analysis. Perceiving this, Dowty's reaction is to complicate the account by invoking the apparatus of possible worlds. Thus, time-relativized Fregean predicates are further relativized to worlds as well as times, and a relation

$$w \overset{t}{=} w'$$

[6] See his 'Toward a Semantic Analysis', and Chapter Three of his book *Word Meaning*.

[7] 'Toward a Semantic Analysis', p. 56. Here and elsewhere in presenting Dowty's ideas I have – I trust fairly – taken the liberty of representing them in terms of the formal framework of the present work.

between two worlds is introduced, and defined as meaning

w and w' are identical at all times up to and including t.

And Dowty's first try at reformulating his analysis of the continuous is to replace it by

$$Cont^*i \quad P_j^{n+1}\text{-ing } x_1 \ldots x_{n-1} t, w \leftrightarrow (\exists t')(t \sqsubset t' \ \&$$
$$(\exists w')(w \stackrel{t}{=} w' \ \& \ V_j^{n+1} t'w')).$$

Thus

(12) Coleridge was writing 'Kubla Khan' (sc. in the actual world, w_a)

now goes over into the formalism as

(12i) $(\exists t)(t < \text{now } \& \ (\exists t')(t \sqsubset t' \ \& \ (\exists w')(w_a \stackrel{t}{=} w' \ \& \ \text{Write(Coleridge, 'Kubla Khan', } t',w'))))$

and hence no longer entails that any time is *actually* a time of Coleridge's writing his epic, *i.e.* that

(13) $(\exists t)(\text{Write(Coleridge, 'Kubla Khan', } t,w_a))$.

But as Dowty came to see,[8] this way of avoiding the problems of the imperfective paradox generates other unacceptable consequences. For suppose Henry is drawing a square, commencing with the base line, and let t be the last moment of his drawing of the base. Since Henry is in fact drawing a square, t falls within a time t' which is, in the actual world, a time of Henry's drawing a square; but there is presumably another world w' in which Henry goes on to draw a triangle rather than a square, so that t also falls within a time t'' which is a time in w' of Henry's drawing a triangle. Hence, by *Cont*i*, when Henry is drawing a square, he is also drawing a triangle. Which he isn't.

Perceiving the unacceptability of modifying *Cont** just to *Cont*i*, Dowty cast about for a more acceptable modification. His next idea is to find an acceptable modification of the form

$$Cont^*ii \quad P_j^{n+1}\text{-ing } x_1 \ldots x_{n-1} t, w \leftrightarrow (\exists t')(t \sqsubset t' \ \&$$
$$(\forall w')(R(w,w',t) \rightarrow V_j^{n+1} \ w't')$$

---

[8] *Word Meaning*, pp. 147–8.

for some reading of '$R(w,w',t)$'. A suggestion with which he toys[9] is to invoke Lewis's key notion of similarity amongst worlds, and to construe $R(w,w',t)$ as holding just in case

$w \doteq w'$ & w and w' are highly similar.

Then (12) will go over as

(12ii) $(\exists t)(t < \text{now}$ & $(\exists t')(t \sqsubset t'$ & $(\forall w')(w_a \doteq w'$ & w_a and w' are highly similar $\rightarrow$ Write(Coleridge, 'Kubla Khan',t',w'))))).

But this won't do, as Dowty sees, since on this construal of the key relation we have $R(w,w,t)$ for each w and t, hence in particular $R(w_a,w_a,t)$ for each t; so the crucial entailment from (12ii) to (13) remains unblocked. Which brings Dowty to his final proposal:[10] to adopt *Cont*$*ii$ whilst construing $R(w,w',t)$ as obtaining just in case

$w \doteq w'$ & $(\forall w'')(w \doteq w'' \rightarrow$ things after t in w' develop at least as compatibly with events before t as they do in w'').

What he seems to miss is – as Parsons pointed out in a review listed in the Bibliography – that this proposal fails for much the same reason as its predecessor did. For obviously $w_a \doteq w_a$; and for any time t, it is hard to see how any course of events after t could be more 'compatible' (in any sense of that vague term) with events after t than is the course of events which actually unfolded in the real world. So on this construal too of the key relation, we have $R(w_a,w_a,t)$ for each t; and Dowty's final proposal fails like its predecessor to block the critical implication from (12) to (13).

The failure of these doughty efforts to articulate a coherent analysis of the continuous which avoids validating this crucial inference suggests there may after all be no such analysis to be found. Suppose then we stick resolutely with *Cont* unmodified, and deny 'x was V-ing' can ever have been true unless x eventually came to V. Still, we can apparently avoid outright clash with intuition in face of examples like the Coleridge one if

[9] *Word Meaning*, p. 148.
[10] *Word Meaning*, pp. 148–9.

we can find room to maintain that even when x never came to V, a sentence of the form.

(14) x was V-ing when y G-ed

can be true nevertheless (and then explain any willingness we have in such cases to count true the simple 'x was V-ing' as there when context renders it natural to construe the simple sentence as shorthand for some genuine truth of the more complex form[11]). Now of course (10) does have *a* reading in which its 'when' functions purely temporally and is represented in Fregean paraphrase merely by a bound temporal variable, and in this sense it goes over into symbols just as

(14i) $(\exists t)(t < \text{now} \ \& \ \sim V(x,t) \ \& \ (\exists t')(t' \sqsubset t \ \&$
        $V(x,t')) \ \& \ G(y,t))$

and hence entails the simple 'x was V-ing'. So the canvassed strategy must maintain that (14) has another reading, in which its 'when' has some non-purely-temporal sense and in which this does not go through.

The notion that 'when' has a sense beyond the purely temporal one is hardly novel. Classical Latin distinguishes the purely temporal 'cum' from senses which vaguely hint at some more modal connexion by combining it with the indicative only when the purely temporal sense is indicated, and finds itself using the subjunctive most of the time. Indeed, using the English subjunctive is one way of indicating a meaning (14) must bear, if it is to have the reading we need beyond the purely temporal (14i). For transposing (14)'s clauses (preserving signification) and then rendering the first into the subjunctive yields

(14ii) When x would be V-ing, y G-ed.

And interpreting this subjunctive as the 'potential subjunctive' of traditional grammar gives the desired reading.

[11] Actually, (14) is more restricted than it need be; for the simple sentence could be regarded as shorthand for any sentence of the more general form 'x was V-ing when A'. I choose the more specific form to simplify the discussion, but the generalization of my remarks to the less restricted case should be obvious enough.

Carrying this over into the symbolism is more difficult. Supposing the language of base paraphrase enriched with Lewis' connective '□→' to render the subjunctive conditional, I would essay construing (14) in sense (14ii) as

(14iii) $(\exists t)\,(t < \text{now} \;\&\; G(y,t) \;\&\; \sim V(x,t) \;\&\;$
$(\exists t')\,(t \sqsubset t' \;\&\; (\sim G(y,t) \;\square\!\!\rightarrow\; V(x,t'))))$

('some time t earlier than now is a time of y's G-ing, and, though not itself a time of x's V-ing, falls within a time t' which, were t not a time of y's G-ing, would be a time of x's V-ing'). But invoking (14iii) raises a further problem – how are Tarskian methods to be extended to yield an austerely adequate truth-theory for a language containing '□→'?

That is, however, a problem which has to be faced anyway, and which can fairly be set to one side as a major one outside the bounds of this essay. From my programmatic remarks in Chapter One, it will be clear that I would reject the Lewis possible-worlds truth-theory for the connective in question as insufficiently austere for the demands of the theory of sense. Still, it is interesting to note that the Lewis truth-condition for (14) in sense (14iii) is remarkably close to that for which Dowty was apparently striving. Dowty and I agree, in fact, that modal notions must be invoked to combat the imperfective paradox, and disagree only over where they should be applied. He has drawn the moral that continuity itself is a modal notion, but failed to show how this assumption can resolve the problem. I prefer instead to stick with an unmodalised analysis of the continuous, and to seek for resolution of the problem in the way the continuous tenses embed in contexts I diagnose as modally-loaded.[12]

8.   If the last section's way with the imperfective paradox is good, *Cont* survives that paradox's terrors without the need for

---

[12] A sketchy version of the line here run appeared in a footnote in my 'Tense and Continuity', and was replied to by Dowty in *Word Meaning* (p. 189, footnote 10). The bulk of his criticisms mistake my view, understandably given its sketchy presentation. The one which survives (his (3)) apparently denies that any reasonable set of transformations could generate (14) from my (14iii). But even if the point is sound, it will apply only to the rich notion of transformations which applies within the global context of a generative

adjustment, and beside it survives the Preliminary Account of Aristotle's taxonomy of verbs as summarized in the last paragraph of section 5. But the temporal story the Preliminary Account tells of K- and E-verbs permits an illuminating spatial analogy, which by deepening understanding of what the Preliminary Account involves at the same time reveals its limitations.

Suppose that a lump of gold were completely *homogeneous*, so that every three-dimensional area wholly within it was itself a lump of gold. (Real gold is, we know thanks to molecular theory, not homogeneous; but before that theory was developed, it was perfectly reasonable to hold that it was.) Then there would be no lower limit on the spatial extent of a lump of gold – though of course some lower limit would operate on the size of the samples which normal criteria could identify *as* gold, and for samples lower than this minimum we could know, without recourse to sophisticated scientific tests, that an item was a lump of gold only by knowing that it was (or had been) part of a larger lump to which the standard tests could be applied. But even within a homogeneous lump of gold, there is no lump of gold at a *point*; for lumps of gold, even homogeneous gold, must occupy some area, however small, of three-dimensional space.

A homogeneous stuff such as gold (on the present assumption) differs instructively from a substance (*e.g.* a table) in the matter of space occupancy. For while no *point* within a homogeneous lump of gold is occupied by a lump of gold, in general *no* (three-dimensional or other) space within a table is occupied by a table, whereas *every* three-dimensional area within a homogeneous lump of gold is occupied by a lump of gold. For a form of words to encapsulate the difference, we may say that a homogeneous stuff *fills*, whereas a substance *delimits*, the space it occupies.

---

grammar, and does not count against a construal of (14iii) as giving the base paraphrase of (14) within the more local framework of the syntax of the theory of sense – *cf.* p. 10 above.

For further remarks on the themes of this section, see section 3.2 of Vlach's 'The Semantics of the Progressive', a paper which came to my hand just as the final version of this book was leaving for the printer.

Now, taking 'falls' and 'stabs' as paradigms respectively of E- and K-verbs, the views of the Preliminary Account with regard to verbs in these categories can be summed up as the theses that falling *fills time* as a homogeneous stuff fills space, whereas stabbing *delimits time* as a substance delimits space. Thus no moment is a time of falling or of stabbing, just as no point is a place occupied by a lump of gold or a table; for falling and stabbing take time, just as both stuffs and substances take up three-dimensional space. Further, just as in general *no* spatial area within a table is itself an area occupied by a table, so the Preliminary Account holds that no period within a period of stabbing is itself such a period; and just as *every* three-dimensional spatial area within a lump of homogeneous gold is itself such a lump of gold, so every period within a period of falling is itself a period of falling.

9.   But once it is seen that this is indeed the spatial analogy which the Preliminary Account invites, doubts arise about its aptness in all cases. For it is clear that, even continuing to waive the claims of molecular theory and to maintain the homogeneity of stuffs such as gold, various *heterogeneous* stuffs ought also to be recognized. Fruit-cake will serve as an example. Division of a lump of fruit-cake will produce a lump of fruit-cake only until a sample of some minimal size is reached; a mere sultana does not in itself constitute a lump of fruit-cake, and can at best be a part of such a lump. There is indeed no obvious requirement that there should be some *absolute* lower limit on the size of a lump of fruit-cake, as there presumably is on the size of the samples our normal criteria can identify as such lumps, since there is no obvious conceptual bar to supposing that a shrinking machine might miniaturize a sample beyond any limit which might be imposed. But even within a sample of miniaturized fruit-cake there will be areas (*e.g.* one occupied by a miniature sultana) which are not themselves occupied by a lump of fruit-cake; and failing theoretical grounds to the contrary, it is natural to suppose that the minimal lumps of fruit-cake within a sample which *is* on the everyday scale are those of just sufficient size to be recognized as fruit-cake by our normal criteria. The contrast of heterogeneous fruit-cake with homogeneous gold therefore emerges sharply in that whereas

any lump of normal-scale fruit-cake must in principle be directly recognizable as such by means of our normal criteria, there may (as already noted) be genuine samples of gold which, themselves of insufficient size to be recognized directly, can be told as such by our standard criteria only indirectly via the knowledge that they form (or have formed) part of a larger lump to which these tests can be applied.

All of which throws doubt upon the universal applicability of the Preliminary Account's views of E-verbs. For in some cases it seems more apt to compare the structure of an E-verb's period of application with the space-occupancy of a heterogeneous rather than a homogeneous stuff. True, there *are* cases where the analogy with homogeneous stuffs is appropriate: even a microsecond within a period of falling is plausibly reckoned as itself genuinely a period of falling, even though it can be told as such by means of normal empirical criteria only indirectly, via the knowledge that it does indeed come within some wider period long enough for those criteria to be applied. 'Falls' we may therefore classify as a *homogeneous E-verb*, grouping it with *e.g.* 'moves', 'ponders', and 'blushes'. But an example like 'chuckles' provides a case more naturally conceived on the analogy of a heterogeneous stuff, since any sounds emitted in a microsecond during a period of chuckling (at the normal rate) hardly constitute chuckling themselves, but rather appear to stand to chuckling as a sultana might stand to fruit-cake, *viz.* as at best falling within some period of chuckling though themselves occupying a time too short to constitute such a period. So, though there is no need to be committed to a lower limit on the length of a possible period of chuckling (since the rate of chuckling can conceivably be increased just as fruit-cake can be miniaturized), within any period of chuckling there will be minimal periods of chuckling, and it is natural to identify the minimal periods of a chuckling carried out at the normal rate with those which everyday empirical criteria can identify as such. These affinities between the way chuckling fills time and a heterogeneous stuff fills space suggest we should classify 'chuckles' as a *heterogeneous E-verb*, grouping it with *e.g.* 'giggles', 'talks', 'walks', and 'strokes (the dog)'; and the Preliminary Account, while now seen to provide in Postulate 3 an explication of the logical properties of *homogeneous* E-verbs, requires a supplementary explication of the properties of the important class of heterogeneous E-verbs thus distinguished.

To obtain such an explication, we are best advised to begin by stating more formally a condition definitive of the way heterogeneous stuffs fill the space they occupy. To which end, let us first single out spatial *areas* from more general spatial *places* in much the same way as temporal periods were earlier distinguished from times in general – any continuous volume of space down to the limiting case of a point is a place, whereas only places more extensive than points count as areas; and, where S is a stuff, let an S-place (or area) be a place (or area) occupied by a lump of S. Then the heterogeneous stuffs S are, it seems, those that meet this *Spatial Heterogeneity Condition*:

(i) any S-place is an S-area

(ii) any S-area A falls (spatially) within (though perhaps not properly within) some area A' such that

(a) A' is S-maximal (*i.e.* an S-area falling properly within no further S-area)

(b) some area within A' is S-minimal (*i.e.* an S-area within which no further S-area falls)

(c) any area within A' is an S-area iff there is within it some S-minimal area.

With this Condition at hand, the desired explication of heterogeneous E-predicate ought to emerge by translating from its spatial vocabulary into the temporal. But that in turn needs some preliminary definition; so I define

(D) t is maximal w.r.t. a set z of times

$$(\mathrm{Max}(t,z)) . \leftrightarrow . t \in z \ \& \ \sim(\exists t')(t \sqsubset t' \ \& \ t' \in z)$$

(D2) t is minimal w.r.t. a set z of times

$$(\mathrm{Min}(t,z)) . \leftrightarrow . t \in z \ \& \ \sim(\exists t')(t' \sqsubset t \ \& \ t' \in z)$$

and further abbreviate by the definition-schemata

[I] $\mathrm{Max}_{V_j^n}(t) \leftrightarrow \mathrm{Max}(t,\{t' \mid V_j^n t'\})$

[II] $\mathrm{Min}_{V_j^n}(t) \leftrightarrow \mathrm{Min}(t,\{t' \mid V_j^n t'\})$.

Utilizing these definitions, we arrive finally at an explication of the heterogeneous E-predicates, by translation into temporal terms of the Spatial Heterogeneity Condition; P_j^n is a heterogeneous E-predicate provided it meets

Postulate 5 $V_j^n t \rightarrow \text{Per}(t)$ &

$$(\exists a)(\text{Max}_{V_j^n}(a \ \& \ t \sqsubseteq a \ \& \ (\exists b)(\text{Min}_{V_j^n}(b) \ \&$$

$$b \sqsubseteq a) \ \& \ (\forall c)(c \sqsubset a \rightarrow (V_j^n c \leftrightarrow$$

$$(\exists b)(\text{Min}_{V_j^n}(b) \ \& \ b \sqsubseteq c))))$$

So, for example, what makes 'Chuckle' (or 'Ch', for brevity) a heterogeneous E-predicate is its obedience to the postulate

Postulate 5a $\text{Ch}(x,t) \ . \rightarrow \text{Per}(t)$ &

$$(\exists a)(\text{Max}_{\text{Ch}(x)}(a) \ \& \ t \sqsubseteq a \ \&$$

$$(\exists b)(\text{Min}_{\text{Ch}(x)}(b) \ \& \ b \sqsubseteq a \ \&$$

$$(\forall c)(c \sqsubset a \rightarrow (\text{Ch}(x,c) \leftrightarrow$$

$$(\exists b)(\text{Min}_{\text{Ch}(x)}(b) \ \& \ b \sqsubseteq c))))$$

where by the definition-schemata [I] and [II] we have

$$\text{Max}_{\text{Ch}(x)}(t) \leftrightarrow \text{Max}(t,\{t' | \text{Ch}(x,t')\})$$

$$\text{Min}_{\text{Ch}(x)}(t) \leftrightarrow \text{Min}(t,\{t' | \text{Ch}(x,t')\}).$$

An obvious difficulty in accepting this as an explication of the logical properties of heterogeneous E-verbs is that it fails to provide for the characteristic entailment, shared by all E-verbs, from 'x is V-ing' to 'x has V-ed'; for, e.g. Postulate 5a allows that there should be a first minimal period within any period of x's chuckling, hence that there should be some absolutely first period which is a time of x's chuckling – and at any time within that period it will on the present elucidation of the tenses be true that x is chuckling, but false that he has chuckled. This difficulty is endemic to the conception of heterogeneous E-verbs as temporal analogues of heterogeneous stuffs, and cannot be avoided by modifying or augmenting the postulate which gives rise to it. But there is no cause for undue concern, provided the natural assumption be made that the minimal periods of chuckling within a piece of normal-rate chuckling are the least times of chuckling so discernible by normal empirical criteria. For then it will at least remain true that no speaker will be in a position *warrantably to assert* that x is chuckling until, some minimal period of chuckling having passed and been recognized, it is true that x has chuckled; so although on the present view it must be denied that there is a genuine entailment from 'x is V-ing' to 'x has V-ed' for heterogeneous E-verbs, at least it is clear why it should have seemed plausible for theorists to have held that there is.

10.   The distinction of two classes of E-verbs just made has its ramifications too for the theory of the nature of K-verbs enshrined in the Preliminary Account. For the strategy pursued in arriving at that theory assumed that there would be some one property characteristic of E-verbs, an explication of which would enable identification of an opposed property which could be taken as characteristic of K-verbs; but now it has emerged that the assumption underlying this strategy is false, and that the Preliminary Account should be seen as opposing K-verbs, not to E-verbs generally, but more particularly to *homogeneous* E-verbs. So, without denying the *prima facie* plausibility of the earlier explication, the possibility arises of an alternative and perhaps more satisfactory theory which will oppose K-verbs rather to the *heterogeneous* E-verbs.

The claims, such as they are, of spatial analogy in fact point towards this second alternative. For when I originally compared the way K-verbs according to the Preliminary Account delimit time with the way substances delimit space, my ground was that a substance generally inhabits a space no area within which is occupied by a substance of the same sort. But as the hedge in 'generally' indicates, the analogy is really less than perfect – a table, for example, can be made up of a number of smaller ones slotted together. So a truly accurate account of the way substances delimit space should allow for the possibility that sometimes a substance can inhabit an area which itself contains some areas occupied by substances of the same kind. What remains true is that not *every* area within an area occupied by a substance can be occupied by a substance of the same kind. Thus substances, like heterogeneous stuffs, contain *minimal* areas of occupancy by substances of the same kind; where they differ from such stuffs is in containing areas which embrace a minimal area yet fail to be occupied by a substance of the given kind. Thus the natural spatial contrast, properly construed, is between substances and heterogeneous stuffs. So if the spatial analogy which the Preliminary Account suggested is to be carried through in its fine detail, we should expect to prefer a theory of K-verbs which opposes them to the heterogeneous E-verbs, rather than to the homogeneous ones after the fashion of the Preliminary Account itself.

In search of such a theory, we begin with the observation that (where S is now a *substance-kind*, and an S-place (area) is a place (area) occupied by an instance of S), a condition definitive of the way substances delineate space can be obtained from the Spatial Heterogeneity Condition by substituting for clause (ii) (c) the requirement

(c′) for any S-minimal area A'' properly within A', there is an area within which A'' falls, and which falls within A', but which is not an S-area.

By constructing a temporal analogue of the condition thus obtained, we therefore arrive at a view of K-verbs which at once opposes them to heterogeneous E-verbs and maintains a full analogy with the space-occupancy of substances, *viz.* the view that the K-predicates P_j^n are those meeting

Postulate 6 $V_j^n t. \rightarrow .\ \mathrm{Per}(t)\ \&$

$(\exists a)(\mathrm{Max}_{V_j^n}(a)\ \&\ t \sqsubseteq a\ \&\ (\exists b)(\mathrm{Min}_{V_j^n}(b)\ \&$

$b \sqsubseteq a)\ \&$

$(\forall c)(\mathrm{Min}_{V_j^n}(c)\ \&\ c \sqsubset a \rightarrow (\exists d)(c \sqsubset d\ \&$

$d \sqsubset a\ \&\ \sim V_j^n d)))$.

Putting the matter more wordily, what this postulate requires of a K-verb V is that a period t of x's V-ing should be contained in a maximal period a of x's V-ing, and contain a minimal period b of x's V-ing; with the further proviso that any such minimal period b fall within some subinterval of the maximal a which is *not* a time of x's V-ing. Notice that this condition *allows* that t be identical both with the containing maximal a and with the contained minimal b, and that were we to *require* that these be identical we would be back with the Preliminary Account's guiding view of K-predicates, Postulate 4. The new

Postulate 6 is thus a more complex but weaker requirement on K-predicates than that previously imposed. The question which arises is therefore whether (apart from the dubious desire to maintain the spatial analogy point for point) there is any need to construe K-predicates according to this new and laxer standard, rather than to cleave to the simplicity of the older story.

11. Surprisingly enough, such a need does arise, out of complexities connected with the continuous tenses of quantified sentences containing K-verbs. A sentence like

(15) John is polishing all (the) boots

can be true (as I shall say) *consecutively* and not just *simultaneously*; that is, it can be true at any time during a performance in which John systematically works his way through a heap of boots, polishing each in turn, and does not require that any time of his polishing one boot should be a time of his polishing any other (a feat presumably impossible, assuming John to have the normal complement of limbs). Now the truth of (15) on the present account of the continuous tenses requires that there is a time t such that now $\sqsubset t$ and

(16) $(\forall y)(\text{Boot}(y) \rightarrow \text{Polish}(\text{John},y,t))$.

Hence we must suppose that K-predicates so relate times to individuals that there is such a time, even when (15) is consecutively true. This is ensured by the supposition that the K-predicates P_j^n meet a further requirement, namely that we have (for each i such that $1 \leqslant i < \text{n}$)

Postulate 7 $(\forall x_i)(\text{A}(x_i) \rightarrow (\exists t_1)(t_1 \sqsubset t \ \& \ V_j^n t_1)) \ \&$

$(\forall t_2)(\text{Mom}(t_2) \ \& \ t_2 \sqsubset t \rightarrow$

$(\exists x_i)(\exists t_3)(t_2 \sqsubset t_3 \ \& \ \text{A}(x_i) \ \& \ V_j^n t_3))$

$. \rightarrow . \ (\forall x_i)(\text{A}(x_i) \rightarrow V_j^n t)$

where x_i is the i-th variable in the standard ordering and $\text{A}(x_i)$ is any formula containing x_i free. (Recall, in construing this formalism, that x_i also by our syntactic conventions occurs as the i-th free variable in V_j^n.) For as an instance of this schema we have

Postulate 7a $(\forall y)(\text{Boot}(y) \rightarrow (\exists t_1)(t_1 \sqsubset t \,\&$

$$\text{Polish}(x,y,t_1))) \,\& \,(\forall t_2)(\text{Mom}(t_2) \,\& \,t_2 \sqsubset t \rightarrow$$

$$(\exists y)(\exists t_3)(t_2 \sqsubset t_3 \,\& \,\text{Boot}(y) \,\&$$

$$\text{Polish}(x,y,t_3))) \,. \rightarrow . \,(\forall y)(\text{Boot}(y) \rightarrow$$

$$\text{Polish}(x,y,t))$$

which ensures that even when John's polishing of the boots is consecutive, there will be a time *–viz.* the time stretching from his applying the first lick of polish to the first boot, up to his laying aside of the last – which meets the condition imposed in (16) (assuming, as seems reasonable, that we are prepared to count any moment in a pause between his laying aside the n-th boot and his first brush-stroke on the $(n+1)$th as belonging either to the time of his polishing the n-th boot, or to that of his polishing the $(n+1)$th).

Postulate 7, needed for these reasons, is of course straightforwardly incompatible with the old account of K-verbs as enshrined in Postulate 4; for the very reason it has been invoked is to ensure the existence of a time t such that

$$(\forall y)(\text{Boot}(y) \rightarrow \text{Polish}(j,y,t))$$

so that for any boot b_i

$$\text{Polish}(j,b_i,t)$$

in circumstances where t is not a minimal period of John's polishing b_i, *i.e.* for some time $t' \sqsubset t$

$$\text{Polish}(j,b_i,t')$$

in contradiction to Postulate 4. This possibility is, however, allowed by Postulate 6, whose laxer conditions appear indeed to describe quite succinctly the structure of the more complex periods of application of K-verbs to which we are now committed. The latter postulate should accordingly be preferred in the final reckoning; K-predicates are thus to be construed as contrasting with heterogeneous rather than homogeneous E-predicates, and the spatial analogy with substances is vindicated in the fuller detail.

12. Some puzzles connected with Postulate 7, however, survive this decision. One of these is that if the time t of John's whole consecutive boot-polishing performance is to count as a time of his polishing any boot b_i, then by the favoured account of the continuous tenses, at *any* moment within t it is true that John is polishing boot b_i – even *e.g.* at a moment when he has laid b_i aside as finished, and begun applying polish to boot b_{i+1}. This may seem just wrong; for (Case 1) no *observer* of John's performance can legitimately assert that he is polishing boot b_i when he has manifestly moved on to boot b_{i+1}. On the other hand, not all the linguistic evidence is hostile to the present consequence. Thus (Case 2) a hotel-guest, having left his boots out for cleaning the previous night, may enquire of a maid as to their whereabouts, and be informed that John is currently cleaning them; and for the maid's answer to be honest, it is not necessary that John actually be operating on the boots in question, but will suffice that they be part of the heap of guests' boots he is currently working his way through as part of his duties.

The solution to this difficulty lies in accepting the consequence of the proposed semantic account that the assertions of both observer and maid are literally true, but appealing to pragmatic conventions governing assertion to contrast the illegitimacy of the former with the acceptability of the latter. For there is a general duty of the speakers of a language (based on the mutual interest of all concerned) not to mislead their audience, hence to base their assertions on the most specific information to which they have access. So we may posit a Principle of Strongest Assertion governing the conditions under which speakers are to assert continuous-tensed sentences containing K-verbs V, dictating (roughly) that a speaker should not assert that x is V-ing merely on the basis of a belief that the current moment falls within some *non*-minimal period of x's V-ing, if he also has grounds for believing that the current moment does *not* fall within a minimal period of x's V-ing. The observer of John's polishing is, accordingly, not entitled to assert that John is polishing boot b_i on the basis of his belief that the current moment falls within a time t of John's polishing of every boot (even though the sentence thereby asserted would be literally true), since the testimony of his senses informs him that the current moment falls within a minimal period of John's polishing of boot b_{i+1} but not of boot b_i; whereas the maid of Case 2, who presumably lacks any knowledge of the minimal periods within the non-minimal time t of John's polishing every boot, is thereby entitled to use her less specific belief about the wider period in framing a continuous-tensed assertion which is not just literally true, but sanctioned by the conventions of assertion.

Appeal to this pragmatic principle also enables us to see how the common slogan that, for K-verbs V, 'x is V-ing' entails 'x has not V-ed', is to be interpreted on the present account of K-verbs. It can indeed no longer be claimed, as it was in section 6, that the insight underlying this slogan is that whenever the current moment falls within a time t of x's V-ing, no time earlier than the current moment and within t is a time of x's V-ing; for as we have seen, we must now allow that if John polishes the boots consecutively, a time t_i of his polishing boot b_i can precede the current moment and both nevertheless fall within a time t which, as a time of John's polishing every boot, is a time of his polishing boot b_i. Nevertheless, it remains true that a totally informed observer, operating in accordance with the Principle of Strongest Assertion, will not *assert* that x is V-ing unless the current moment falls within some *minimal* time of x's V-ing, in which no time earlier than the current moment can be a time of x's V-ing; and it seems reasonable to offer this in explication of the standard slogan.

13. We have reached at last a Final Account of Aristotle's taxonomy of verbs. This final theory is a fairly far-reaching revision, through spatial analogy, of the first attempt of the Preliminary Account: whilst S-verbs are still to be explicated by positing S-predicates meeting the Preliminary Account's Postulate 1, E-verbs now divide into the homogeneous and the heterogeneous, with Postulate 3 explicating the properties of predicates underlying verbs of the former class, and Postulate 5 those of predicates underlying verbs of the latter; and K-verbs are now construed as those whose underlying predicates satisfy

Postulate 6 rather than the old Postulate 4, with Postulate 7 as an additional condition governing at least some of them. It will be noted that, of the *prima facie* entailments used to draw up the original intuitive classification, only that of homogeneous E-verbs has been ultimately vindicated as genuine. But appeal to pragmatics enables the ground for the supposed entailments of the other cases to be understood. And it is commonplace anyway for a philosophical theory to refine the intuitions which give it rise.

Postscript to Chapter 3

A Theory of Times

Primitives: identity and temporal precedence. *Defined* predicates are introduced as follows (read 'Lin(t,t')' as 't and t' are linearly related'; 'Ol(t,t')' as 't overlaps with t''; and 'Str(t,x,y)' as 't stretches from x to y'):

(Df 1) $\text{Lin}(t,t') \leftrightarrow t < t' \lor t = t' \lor t' < t.$

(Df 2) $\text{Ol}(t,t') \leftrightarrow {\sim}\text{Lin}(t,t')\ \&$

$\qquad (\exists x)(x < t\ \&\ {\sim}x < t' . \lor . t < x\ \&\ {\sim}t' < x).$

(Df 3) $t \sqsubset t' \leftrightarrow \text{Ol}(t,t')\ \&\ {\sim}\text{Ol}(t',t).$

(Df 4) $t \sqsubseteq t' \leftrightarrow t \sqsubset t' \lor t = t'.$

(Df 5) $\text{Mom}(t) \leftrightarrow {\sim}(\exists t')\text{Ol}(t',t).$

(Df 6) $\text{Per}(t) \leftrightarrow (\exists t')(\text{Mom}(t')\ \&\ t' \sqsubset t).$

(Df 7) $\text{Str}(t,x,y) \leftrightarrow x \sqsubset t\ \&\ y \sqsubset t\ \&\ (\forall z)(z < t \rightarrow z < x . \&$

$\qquad . t < z \rightarrow y < z).$

(Df 8) $\text{OF}(t) \leftrightarrow \text{Per}(t)\ \&\ (\forall t')(\text{Mom}(t')\ \&\ t' \sqsubset t$

$\qquad \rightarrow (\exists t'')(t'' \sqsubset t\ \&\ t'' < t')).$

(Df 9) $\text{OE}(t) \leftrightarrow \text{Per}(t)\ \&\ (\forall t')(\text{Mom}(t')\ \&\ t' \sqsubset t$

$\qquad \rightarrow (\exists t'')(t'' \sqsubset t\ \&\ t' < t'')).$

As *axioms* based on a conception of time as stretching continuously in both directions, take the following:

(A1) $\text{Per}(t) \vee \text{Mom}(t)$.

(A2) $(\forall x)(x < t \leftrightarrow x < t' \,.\, \& \,.\, t < x \leftrightarrow t' < x) \rightarrow t = t'$

(A3) $t < t' \rightarrow \sim t' < t$.

(A4) $t < t' \,\&\, t' < t'' \rightarrow t < t''$.

(A5) $\sim(\exists t)(\forall t')(\text{Mom}(t') \,\&\, t \neq t' \rightarrow t' < t)$.

(A6) $\sim(\exists t)(\forall t')(\text{Mom}(t') \,\&\, t \neq t' \rightarrow t < t')$.

(A7) $(\text{Mom}(t) \vee \text{Mom}(t')) \,\&\, t < t' \,.\, \rightarrow \,.\, (\exists t'')(t < t'' \,\& \, t'' < t')$.

(A8) $x < y \rightarrow (\exists t)\text{Str}(t,x,y)$.

(A9) $(\exists t)(\forall t')(t' \sqsubset t \leftrightarrow a < t' \,\&\, t' < b)$

(A10) $t < t' \,\&\, \text{OE}(t) \,\&\, \text{OF}(t') \rightarrow (\exists a)(t < a \,\&\, a < t')$.

4

Events

1. It is time now to cash in some promissory notes, by showing how the machinery of states of affairs can combine with Aristotle's partition of verbs to yield the theory of events which I set myself at the end of my first chapter to find.

2. Roughly speaking, the leading idea of the theory I wish to advance is, as earlier announced, that events should be construed as a species of obtaining states of affairs, *i.e.* of facts. Put more precisely so as to take account of the language-relativity inherent in the construction of states of affairs developed in the second chapter, the idea is accordingly that the events of which we speak in English (my paradigm natural language) can be identified with certain of the states of affairs posited by a suitable first-order language *LE* apt for Fregean formalization of ordinary non-event-invoking English talk of persons and their actions, and of substances and their states and changes. But why think any such identification remotely plausible?

Typically, the singular-terms of English which by the lights of intuitive semantics 'designate events' take the form of descriptions. (True, proper names do occasionally figure in the role, *e.g.* in the designation of hurricanes. But Russell's view of ordinary-language names as truncated descriptions is at its strongest in application to these rare cases.) Such descriptions moreover typically take a standard form: they are formed by normalization of quasi-sentential verbal expressions, either employing outright gerund forms of the verb – 'the sinking of the *Tirpitz*', 'Brutus' stabbing of Caesar' – or, when the vocabulary happens to supply them, idiomatic alternatives to the gerund – thus, 'Etna's eruption' for 'the erupting of Etna', 'Cicero's denunciation of Catiline' for 'Cicero's denouncing of Catiline'. (Again, there are exceptions, since common nouns like 'funeral' can figure in event-descriptions even though language supplies no obvious candidate verbs of which they can be regarded as nominalizations. But even in these cases it is often plausible to regard the nouns as nominalizations of verbs present in deep structure but prevented by quirks of trans-formation or by haphazard linguistic fashion from appearing on the surface save in their nominalized shape; so that 'Churchill's funeral' can be regarded as being at a deeper level of the form 'the funeraling of Churchill'.) Our standard way of referring to events is thus by means of terms formed by nominalizing sentences; which makes it plausible to think that the events referred to will turn out to be entities whole sentences describe.

But though considerations like these may motivate a picture of events as sentential correlates they fall short of giving a full-fledged rationale for attempting to construe them as states of affairs; for perhaps after all sense can be made of the idea that sentences are systematically correlated with other entities besides – propositions, maybe – and events are best regarded as sentential correlates of one of these further sorts. To close the gap, we must appeal to some further features of our intuitive understanding of the nominalizations we use to single out events: that we allow that coextensive singular-terms are intersubstitutible within such nominalizations without damage to the denotation of the whole, yet deny that nominalizations are found to be codesignative merely on the ground that they embed coextensive verbs. (Thus we count Diana's marrying Charles the same event as her marrying the Prince of Wales, but would continue to deny its identity with her embracing him even in the unlikely case that all and only embracings were between the married.) Such striking parallels between the way

an event-designation relates to its event and the manner in
which a sentence relates to the state of affairs it describes
establish surely that if any view of events as sentential
correlates will work, it must be that which depicts events as in
the category of states of affairs.

3.   But if events (spoken of in English) are states of affairs
(posited by some suitable underlying first-order language *LE*),
just which of the states of affairs *LE* posits deserve the accolade
of eventhood? First, events are one and all *facts*: for if there is
no obvious need to countenance nonoccurrent events, and if
events are to be states of affairs, then to occur is for them
presumably the same as to obtain. But further, events must be
changes: Brutus' being noble is no event, in contrast with his
chuckling or his stabbing Caesar. And events must not just be
changes, but be *temporally continuous* changes: for Reagan's
eating breakfast and his eating dinner are both events, but
there is no one event which is his eating of both. And finally,
the change associated with an event must be continuously
manifested *in some one object* – though both Jack's climbing
Snowdon and Jill's climbing Everest are events, even if the two
are so intimately connected temporally as to be simultaneous
there is no counting Jack's climbing the one and Jill's climbing
the other as a single event, since no one substance, whether
climbing or clambered upon, figures in both components.
(Contrast the climbing of Snowdon by Jack and by Jill, which
may in appropriate temporal circumstances qualify as the one
event, thanks to Snowdon's patient involvement in the two
subsidiary happenings.) So the events *LE* posits are, it seems,
those of its facts which constitute temporally continuous
changes manifested in some one object. Call that the 'Guiding
View'. Its informal language cries out for explication.
   The key to the explication I proffer, hardly concealed by the
emphases of the last chapter, is that first-order languages *L*
generally (and *LE* amongst them) record 'changes' by the
primitive predicates they deploy as K- and E-predicates,
counting such predicates as those which, on *L*'s designated
model, satisfy either the last chapter's Postulate 6 or else one of
its Postulates 3 or 5. Taking that point, an *atomic* state of
affairs posited by first-order *L* should count as, according to *L*,

eventlike – *i.e.* as a state which, by L's lights, need but obtain to be an event – just in case it is of the form $<\text{Int}_L(P^n),b_1 \ldots b_{n-1},t>$, for some K- or E-predicate P^n of L; for according to L, for such a state of affairs to obtain is for the change P^n records to be manifested throughout t in $b_1 \ldots b_{n-1}$. And moving beyond the merely atomic, what the Guiding View suggests is that L's eventlike states of affairs generally be taken as those which either are, or else are equivalent to, certain *sets* of its atomic eventlike states of affairs – those sets, namely, all of whose members are of the form

$$<\text{Int}_L(P^n),b_1 \ldots b_{m-1},c,b_{m+1} \ldots b_{n-1},t>$$

for some shared P^n, c, t, and m less than n. For if any such set of states of affairs obtains – *i.e.*, if all members of any such set obtain – then, according to L, the change P^n records is throughout t continuously manifested in the object c.

Cleaning this up into a series of definitions apt for formal rendition in the metalanguage ML in which the theory of L's states of affairs is constructed, we define accordingly:

[D1] ξ is *primarily eventlike$_L$* $\leftrightarrow \xi \subseteq \Sigma_L^{AT}$ & $\xi \neq \emptyset$ & $(\exists P^n)(\exists c)(\exists t)(\exists m > n)(P^n$ is a primitive K- or E-predicate of L & $(\forall \zeta)(\zeta \in \xi \rightarrow (\exists b_1) \ldots (\exists b_{m-1})$ $(\exists b_{m+1}) \ldots (\exists b_{n-1})(\zeta = <\text{Int}_L(P^n),b_1 \ldots b_{m-1},c,$ $b_{m+1} \ldots b_{n-1},t>)))$

[D2] ξ is *eventlike$_L$* $\leftrightarrow (\exists \xi')(\xi'$ is primarily eventlike$_L$ & $\xi \approxeq \xi')$

[D3] ξ is an *event$_L$* $\leftrightarrow \xi$ is eventlike$_L$ & ξ obtains$_L$.

Notice how on this implementation, L's events are circumscribed without need for prior definition of its *atomic* eventlike states. Still, these emerge as eventlike nevertheless, since any such atomic state of affairs is equivalent to its unit set, which counts trivially as eventlike under [D1].

Before turning to illustration and evaluation of the explication thus arrived at, a formal flaw remains to be rectified. For the definitions just given assume that the sets of states of affairs which [D1] characterizes as primarily eventlike are themselves states of affairs posited by L – else *e.g.* [D2] will fail to do its work, since $\approxeq$ is defined only over Σ_L. Yet clause (iii) of the definition of Σ_L (p. 40) which admits sets of states of affairs into

Σ_L is subject to a cardinality requirement which primarily eventlike sets may fail. Still, clause (iii)'s cardinality proviso has done little work in the foregoing, its sole rationale being to prevent Σ_L from becoming too unnecessarily or uncontrollably large; and now that we have a motive for doing so, no evident harm is done if we suppose it relaxed to the extent of allowing *all* sets of *atomic* states of affairs to count as states of affairs themselves, thus evading the formal difficulty.

4.　Turning now to a case to illustrate the foregoing formalism and facilitate a check of its adequacy to intuition, suppose that some time t_0 is a time of Shem's hitting Shaun, and of Clem's hitting him too; and that throughout t_0 Shaun yammered whilst Clem pondered (perhaps debating the morality of his action). Then, apparently we English speakers are happy to acknowledge the occurrence in the circumstances of a hitting of Shaun by Shem, a hitting of Shaun by Clem, a yammering of Shaun, and a pondering by Clem. And our intuitions are to this extent at least preserved by the explication, assuming that the language *LE* whose posited events we identify with those spoken in English is sensible enough to contain a 3-place K-predicate 'Hit' and 2-place E-predicates 'Yammer' and 'Ponder', respectively of heterogeneous and homogeneous variety. For then the states of affairs

$$\eta_1 = <\text{Int}_{LE}(\text{'Hit'}), \text{Shem}, \text{Shaun}, t_0>$$
$$\eta_2 = <\text{Int}_{LE}(\text{'Hit'}), \text{Clem}, \text{Shaun}, t_0>$$
$$\eta_3 = <\text{Int}_{LE}(\text{'Yammer'}), \text{Shaun}, t_0>$$
$$\eta_4 = <\text{Int}_{LE}(\text{'Ponder'}), \text{Clem}, t_0>$$

all count under the recommended explication as events *LE* posits apt for identification with those intuition acknowledges.

In identifying those intuitive events with the set-theoretic structures η_1–η_4, the present explication is hardly novel. Precisely the same identification has been urged by a number of previous writers, in particular Jaegwon Kim, Alvin Goldman, R.M. Martin and N.L. Wilson[1], whose work provides the foundation upon which the current analysis builds. Where the

---

[1] See the papers by Kim, Martin and Wilson listed in the Bibliography; and Goldman's *Theory*, especially Chapter One.

present explication does differ from these predecessors is in invoking the Aristotelian machinery of *energeia* and *kinesis* to separate atomic events like $\eta_1 - \eta_4$ from mere facts. And it differs too in the way it systematically extends the realm of events beyond the atomic into the complex.

For in addition to countenancing η_1 and η_2 as separate hittings of Shaun respectively performed by Shem and Clem, the present explication also counts amongst *LE*'s events their pair set $\{\eta_1, \eta_2\}$ – a hitting of Shaun by Shem and Clem (and a hitting of Shaun by all the O'Gradys, if Shem and Clem exhaust the clan). Indeed, provided *LE*'s K-predicate 'Hit' meets the last chapter's Postulate 7 (p. 76), it would continue to countenance this more complex occurrence even in somewhat looser temporal circumstances than those so far envisaged. Thus, suppose Clem began his battery upon Shaun just a little later than did Shem and continued it somewhat longer, so that the time t_1 of Clem's hitting coincides in its forward portion only with t_0's latter end; and let $t_0{}^{\wedge}t_1$ be the time running from t_0's lower bound through to the upper bound of t_1. Then in virtue of Postulate 7, both of the states of affairs

$$\eta_5 = \,< \mathrm{Int}_{LE}(\text{'Hit'}), \text{Shem}, \text{Shaun}, t_0{}^{\wedge}t_1 >$$
$$\text{and} \quad \eta_6 = \,< \mathrm{Int}_{LE}(\text{'Hit'}), \text{Clem}, \text{Shaun}, t_0{}^{\wedge}t_1 >$$

must count amongst *LE*'s facts, and by our definitions amongst its events as well. But then under those definitions their pair set $\{\eta_5, \eta_6\}$ counts as a further event, and a hitting of Shaun by both Shem and Clem emerges even in the revised temporal circumstances. Events, then, under the proposed explication can combine to form further ones, when their constituents are sufficiently similar and temporal circumstances are propitious; but they do not so combine promiscuously – the explication acknowledges no single event of Clem's hitting and his pondering. All of which sits well enough with the Guiding View it attempts to encapsulate, and with the intuitions of at least one man (me).

Further, even if Shaun pacifistically declined to retaliate to the assault our example envisages, so that *LE* countenances Shaun's non-hitting of Shem $= \,< \sim, \mathrm{Int}_{LE}(\text{'Hit'}), \text{Shaun}, \text{Shem}, t_0 >$ as a fact, the explication refuses that fact the accolade of eventhood. Indeed, it is provable quite generally that if any state of affairs ξ is eventlike, its negate $<\sim,\xi>$ cannot be,[2] so that the explication refuses to accord the status of an event to any fact which merely reports the non-occurrence of something which would (had it occurred) have deserved that title. In one good sense of the phrase, then, the explication declines to countenance 'negative events'.

It will, despite my best efforts, hardly have escaped attention that the features of the present account just noted with an air of detached abstraction – that it accommodates the discriminate summing of events, whilst eschewing negative ones – are two of those singled out back in Chapter One's section 8 as desirable in a theory of events sufficient to underpin Davidson's view of mode adverbs as event-predicates. The connexion made, it is further clear that by identifying events with set-theoretically-constructed states of affairs, the account we have reached possesses other features too deemed desirable in the theory then anticipated. For we are in a position now to give precise identity-criteria for events (events are identical when the sets with which they are identified have the same members), and to answer in sharp set-theoretic terms questions which arise concerning the relation of Shem to his hitting Shaun, or the relation of the latter to the more complex hitting of Shaun by Shem and Clem. All of which suggests we are in a position now to return to the adverbial themes of the first chapter, and to seek to combine events as now explicated with a Davidsonian construal of mode adverbs as predicates upon them. But before turning to the problems that combination may raise, I shall devote the rest of this chapter to turning objections which arise to my account of events in relative independence of Davidson's adverbial views.

5.   One such objection comes from Davidson himself,[3] and

---

[2] Observe first that if ζ is primarily eventlike$_L$, then (i) $\zeta = \mathrm{Range}_L(\zeta)$, by [D1] and the definition of range (p. 45), and (ii) $\emptyset \notin \zeta$, by [D1]. Now suppose both ξ and $<\sim,\xi>$ eventlike$_L$. Then by [D2] there are primarily eventlike$_L$ ζ, ζ' s.t. $\xi \not\sim \zeta$ and $<\sim,\xi> \not\sim \zeta'$, whence by (i) and the definition of equivalence (p. 45), $\mathrm{Range}_L(\xi) = \zeta$ and $\mathrm{Range}_L(<\sim,\xi>) = \zeta'$. But by the definition of range, either $\emptyset \in \mathrm{Range}_L(\xi)$ or $\emptyset \in \mathrm{Range}_L(<\sim,\xi>)$. Hence either $\emptyset \in \zeta$ or $\emptyset \in \zeta'$; but neither is possible by (ii), since ζ and ζ' are both eventlike$_L$.

[3] See *e.g.* 'Reply to Martin'.

holds that the canvassed theory is hopelessly overstrict in the
way it counts events. For suppose Brutus at t stabbed Caesar,
thereby killing him. Then on the current view, Brutus' stabbing
of Caesar ($= <\text{Int}_{LE}(\text{'Stab'}), \text{Brutus}, \text{Caesar}, t>$) is quite distinct
from his killing of him ($= <\text{Int}_{LE}(\text{'Kill'}), \text{Brutus}, \text{Caesar}, t>$),
since the two differ in first element; yet both preanalytic
intuition and vernacular use urge that the events are identical.
Similarly, intuition and use suggest that in suitable circumstances a particular hand-waving may be a greeting, or a name-
writing a cheque-signing; but the explication I proffer is
evidently bound to count such events as totally distinct, due to
the divergence of their component elements.

I have suggested already (back in Chapter One's eighth
section) that identity-criteria such as Davidson's own which
count pairs of events such as these identical do not obviously sit
easily with the use of events in adverbial analysis, being too
prone to generate such unwanted results as that warnings can
be done uphill or trigger-pullings done with rifles. That point
hardly nullifies the present claims of intuition and usage, but
since intuition and usage are notorious anyway for mistaking
as genuine identities some ersatz substitute it does suggest that
their claims might best be met if some other relation short of
full identity – call it *kinship* – could be defined to hold between
these intimately related events, whilst leaving it open for us to
maintain nevertheless their literal distinctness.

And this can be done easily enough. For, taking causation to
be a relation between events (or, perhaps better, between facts
generally) there is no bar to mimicking Davidson's account of
identity itself, and defining events as akin just in case they share
all causes and effects. The resulting view is not evidently worse
off than Davidson's own in characterizing the relation between
the events of the example and similar pairs, and is better off
overall in having a sharp set-theoretic account of the fundamental relation of identity whilst locating vaguenesses of
Davidsonian identity in a subsidiary relation. (Not, as
Christopher Peacocke pointed out to me, that kinship as
defined will be a *precise* correspondent to Davidsonian
identity; for the language-relativity of the present construction
means presumably that the events quantified over in
characterizing kinship are a more restricted set than those

Davidson quantifies over in circumscribing identity. Rather, kinship stands to Davidsonian identity somewhat as Hilbert-Bernays identity stands to identity proper; but the point has I think little bearing on the ability of the proposed manoeuvre to accommodate the claims of usage and intuition.)

6. Jennifer Hornsby has levelled a different objection to the proposed construction: events cannot be, as it maintains, sets of a certain sort, since 'sets are not the sorts of things to have the properties that the things denoted by the event terms of our language have; and *vice versa*'.[4] To evaluate the criticism, let me distinguish two sorts of potentially troublesome cases – *weak* cases, where identification of events with sets means that events or sets come to be said to have properties we merely had no preanalytic inclination to say they had; and *strong* cases, where the identification licenses our saying that they have properties we hitherto thought we had the best of grounds for saying they actually lacked.

The weak cases pose little problem, finding analogues in the set-theoretic constructions of the natural numbers which I take to be indisputably sound. The event of Plato's running at t, identified by me with a particular set, comes thereby to possess a relational property of which intuition was ignorant (it has Plato as a member of a member of one of its members, to cash n-tuples Kuratowski's way); but so similarly on von Neumann's construction does the number 6 come to have surprising relational properties (such as having 4 as a subset, and 1 as one of its members). Conversely, as Hornsby notes, a particular set (containing t as a member of one of its members) turns out according to me to be Plato's running at t, and hence to have a property intuition thought no set possessed, that of *occurring at* a member of one of its members; but so similarly does the null set turn out according to von Neumann to have the property of being numerically less than 5. One learns something every day.

Biting the bullet thus is hardly possible in troublesome cases of the strong kind, but these are correspondingly harder to

[4] See her *Actions* p. 136; and for development of the criticism, her 'Verbs and Events'.

find. Hornsby's own most convincing example presupposes acceptance of Davidson's construal of mode adverbs as event-predicates, an issue from which the present chapter is meant to abstract. But let us waive that restriction momentarily for the sake of the example, and suppose that Jones buttered the toast in the bathroom. Then, if Davidson's way with mode adverbs is right, some event of Jones' buttering of the toast has the property of being in the bathroom. So if events are sets, some set is in the bathroom. But sets cannot be in bathrooms, since they have no spatio-temporal position at all. My response is to urge that the case teaches merely that the sense in which Jones' buttering of the toast can be in the bathroom is distinct from that in which either Jones or the toast can be in it (though doubtless the event derives its ascribed location in some – not entirely straightforward – way from the position of Jones, the toast, or both). But the non-spatio-temporal nature of sets prohibits their being in bathrooms only in the sense of 'in' appropriate to Jones and the toast, and in the derivative sense of 'in' in which butterings can inhabit bathrooms there is no reason for denying that sets can too.

Further strong cases of the Hornsby kind, it might be thought, arise when modal properties are taken into account. It is of the essence of a set that it has the elements which it does. So in particular, the structure $<\text{Int}_{LE}(\text{'Die'}),\text{Caesar},t_2>$ is essentially connected with its temporal component t_2 (the time, we shall take it, which is in fact the time of Caesar's dying). Yet the event of Caesar's dying is surely not connected *essentially* with t_2, the time of its actual occurrence, since it could (and would, had circumstances been slightly different) have occurred somewhat later than that. Hence Caesar's death is not to be identified with the set-theoretical structure our explication proposes, since the explicating entity has an essential connexion with t_2 which the explicated entity lacks.

But could Caesar's death really have occurred later than t_2? What is of course uncontestably true is that Caesar might have died at a time later than then, *i.e.* that

(1) $(\exists t)(t_2 < t \ \& \ \Diamond \text{Die}(\text{Caesar},t))$.

From this we can quickly derive in the theory of states of affairs that

(2) $(\exists t)(t_2 < t$ & $\Diamond <\mathrm{Int}_{LE}(\text{'Die'}),\mathrm{Caesar},t> \mathrm{obtains}_{LE})$

which is a formal way of saying, under the explication proposed, that

(3) Concerning t_2, Caesar's death could have occurred later than it.

And this is one good sense which can be given to the claim that Caesar's death could have occurred later than t_2, a sense which our explication can accordingly happily embrace. What the objector needs to establish is that the claim also has a further coherent reading

(4) Concerning t_2 and Caesar's death, the latter might have occurred later than the former

in which the event-term has wider scope than the modal operator; and that in this sense too it is either entailed by the uncontroversially true (1), or certified as true on some more devious grounds. For failing this the objection is defused if we maintain that Caesar's death could have occurred before t_2 only in the harmless narrow-scope sense of (3) which our explication easily accommodates.

7.   The objections so far considered have in their various ways fixed upon one principal component of the account of events I offer, namely its use of set-theory and purportedly counter-intuitive consequences with respect to identity or other properties to which events by that use stand committed. The final objection I wish to discuss looks rather at another key thesis of the explication – its notion that the predicates of a language which record changes be construed as those which by the last chapter's lights emerge as its K- and E-predicates.

When that thesis was first advanced four sections back, it was unaccompanied by any attempt at justification. In its support, one might even at this late stage point out that it leads to a picture in which K- and E-predicates play a similar role in individuating time-filling entities (events) as do sortal predicates and mass-terms in individuating space-filling entities (substances and stuffs), and that such a picture is well motivated by the last chapter's detailed charting of the

analogies holding between those spatial predicates and the
temporal ones. But such general considerations as these are
suggestive merely, and the thesis must ultimately depend on
intuition's judging that there are no cases in which evident K-
or E-predicates fail to be reasonably construed as change-
recorders, and no clear cases of change-recorders which escape
classification of either kind. Sustainable though it may be
across the necessarily limited range of examples hitherto
considered, it accordingly remains vulnerable to counter-
example.

And a class of predicates hit upon by the ever-troublesome
Dowty[5] certainly test the thesis. These are predicates encapsulated in English verbs ('lie', 'sit', 'stand', 'rest', 'perch',
'sprawl' etc.) which can be used to ascribe spatial position. For
there is no temptation to think that these predicates, especially
when ascribed to inanimate subjects, in any sense record
changes – the book's lying on the table involves no change in
either book or table. Yet it seems these predicates resist
straightforward classification as S-predicates. For the intuitive
mark of predicates of that ilk (p. 58) is that the verbs they
underlie repudiate the continuous tenses, yet we can happily
say that the underpants *are lying* on the chair or that the
umbrella *is standing* in the hall. The only other option is to
construe them as E-predicates of homogeneous variety,
contradicting the thesis that all such predicates are change-
recorders.

On second thoughts, however, it is not very appealing to
construe predicates of the disputed class as E-predicates. For
so construing them involves, in view of the last chapter's
Postulate 2, adherence to the view that only *periods* should be
viewed as times of the underpants' lying on the chair or the
umbrella's standing in the hall. But the more plausible view is
surely that moments can be such times as well, and that a
period of the underpants' lying on the chair counts as such only
in virtue of its subsidiary moments so counting. Looking at
things this way, we are led by the last chapter's Postulate 1 to
classify predicates of the troublesome class as S-predicates
after all, thus avoiding identifying them as counter-examples to

[5] See *Word Meaning* section 3.8.2 (pp. 173–80).

the projected explication of events; but this still leaves the problem of explaining how these predicates come happily to consort with the continuous tense in a way the last chapter would preclude.[6]

The gist of the last chapter's way with the continuous, enshrined in *Cont*, is to count a time t a time at which x is V-ing just when (i) t is itself not a time of x's V-ing, but (ii) t falls nevertheless within a time of x's V-ing. S-predicates by this account must fail to have true continuous tensings, since the peculiarity of this temporal structure (encapsulated in the last chapter's Postulate 1) precludes simultaneous satisfaction of both (i) and (ii). But now that a class of S-predicates has been identified which apparently accommodates continuous tensing, we might consider revising the old analysis by simply omitting its first conjunct (i). The result would be replacement of *Cont* by the weaker version *Cont**, already noted (p. 64) as Dowty's preferred alternative; indeed, Dowty's chief aim in adverting to the class of predicates which now confront us is to suggest such a motive for favouring his weaker analysis.

But switching to *Cont**, whatever its advantages in dealing with the predicates of the disputed class, has the unfortunate effect of depriving us of any explanation of why S-predicates generally resist the continuous forms. Moreover, as Dowty himself is astute and even-handed enough to note, it is not a manoeuvre which succeeds even in charting precisely the behaviour of the troublesome predicates. For, it seems, we use continuous constructions with these predicates only when ascribing temporary though lasting position to moveable objects, not when recording permanent location. Wagga

---

[6] A similar sticking-point is reached, incidentally, through considering an attempt Dowty makes in speculative mood (*Word Meaning* p. 176) to support the thesis that the predicates in question are after all genuine E-types and that in consequence no moment can be a time of the underpants' lying on the chair. Underpants-in-motion, he suggests, might traverse the chair's upper surface, yet never actually *be lying upon* it. Defending the construal of predicates in the disputed class of type S, we might retort that this shows at best that no moment during the traversal is a time at which 'the underpants are lying on the chair' is truly *sayable*, not that no such moment is a time *of* the underpants' lying on the chair. But the reply needs to be augmented with an account of just when continuous tensings *are* true when predicates of the disputed class are in play; taking us back to the text.

Wagga *lies* on the Murrumbidgee, but we are loth to say it *is lying* there; yet by the lights of *Cont** the latter should be just as true as it is that the underpants are lying on the chair.

In the final analysis, I suggest we do best to cease looking for an integrated account of the continuous which will embrace the idiosyncracies of the predicates in question, and to seek rather to accommodate them as peculiarities of the subject-matter which English has found it convenient to enshrine in an idiom local to those predicates. After all, we spend more time in pursuit of moveable objects such as underpants, umbrellas and car-keys than we care in our loftier moments to contemplate. It would therefore be unsurprising if we had at hand a linguistic device especially tailored to signal the current presence of objects at a location they are likely to occupy for a period of time large enough to be of interest to a prospective seeker, but combined with a warning that the reported location is likely to be less than permanent. Given that the continuous tense of a verb does, by the preferred primary analysis *Cont*, serve at least to mark the presence of a time within a longer period of the verb's application, it would further be natural for that device to take the grammatical form of a continuous tensing of locality-ascribing verbs. And that seems to be the course English takes, adding to the primary semantic role of the grammatical construction of the continuous which *Cont* encapsulates also the secondary function, when applied to location-ascribing S-predicates, of serving as a handy device of the indicated sort. So (to put it roughly), where V is a location-ascribing predicate and p a place ascribed, 'x is V-ing p' comes by an *ad hoc* though convenient rule of English to count as true at t when (a) t falls within some time t' which is a time of x's V-ing p, (b) t' is broad enough to be of interest to a prospective seeker of x, and (c) x does not thoughout its existence V p; where the inclusion of (a) in *Cont* supplies the tenuous connexion between this localized secondary sense of the continuous and its primary one.[7]

---

[7] Notice that this account deals with Dowty's worry concerning the moving underpants, presented in the last footnote; for at any moment during their transit of the chair, the underpants cannot truly be said to be lying upon it, on pain of breach of condition (b).

5

Adverbs Construed

1. With a proper theory of events now to hand, it is time to return to the adverbial themes of the first chapter, and to evaluate the cocktail which results from mixing the explication of events I advocate with the Davidsonian construal of (mode) adverbs as event predicates.

The events of which we speak in English are, by the last chapter's recommendation, to be identified with the events posited by a first-order language *LE* apt for Fregean formalization of non-event-invoking English prattle about agents and their actions, and substances and their states and changes; and the theory of these events is constructed in turn in a metalanguage *MLE* of *LE* adequate for the construction of the states of affairs it posits. The natural starting-point to an evaluation of the cocktail which interests us is therefore to ask how we fare in the attempt to render adverb-containing English sentences in *MLE* – or, more precisely, in *MLE* augmented with appropriate predicates to regiment mode adverbs in Davidsonian style.

Let us use variables 'ξ' 'ξ''', . . . 'ζ', 'ζ''' . . . as variables of *MLE* restricted in their range to members of Σ_{LE}, and 'η', 'η_1' etc. as variables confined more narrowly still to range just over the events *LE* posits (so that sentences of the forms

$$(\exists \eta)(. . . \eta . . .)$$
and $(\forall \eta)(. . . \eta . . .)$

become convenient shorthand ways of saying, respectively

$$(\exists\xi)(\xi \text{ is an event}_{LE} \ \& \ \ldots \xi \ldots)$$
and $(\forall\xi)(\xi \text{ is an event}_{LE} \rightarrow \ldots \xi \ldots).)$

Then, assuming *MLE* to contain event-predicates to regiment mode adverbs corresponding precisely to those Davidson invoked in his own favoured treatment of adverbial sentences, the way is evidently clear to mimic his structures in paraphrasing such sentences into *MLE*. Thus, taking over a batch of examples from the first chapter

(1) Brutus stabbed Caesar violently
(2) Brutus stabbed Caesar with a knife
(3) Brutus stabbed Caesar violently with a knife
(4) Brutus stabbed Caesar with a knife violently

go over into *MLE* as

(1i) $(\exists\eta)(\exists t)(\eta = <\text{Int}_{LE}(\text{'Stab'}),\text{Brutus},\text{Caesar},t> \ \&$
      $\text{Violent}(\eta))$
(2i) $(\exists\eta)(\exists t)(\eta = <\text{Int}_{LE}(\text{'Stab'}),\text{Brutus},\text{Caesar},t> \ \&$
      $(\exists x)(\text{Knife}(x) \ \& \ \text{With}(x,\eta)))$
(3i) $(\exists\eta)(\exists t)(\eta = <\text{Int}_{LE}(\text{'Stab'}),\text{Brutus},\text{Caesar},t> \ \&$
      $\text{Violent}(\eta) \ \& \ (\exists x)(\text{Knife}(x) \ \& \ \text{With}(x,\eta)))$
(4i) $(\exists\eta)(\exists t)(\eta = <\text{Int}_{LE}(\text{'Stab'}),\text{Brutus},\text{Caesar},t> \ \&$
      $(\exists x)(\text{Knife}(x) \ \& \ \text{With}(x,\eta)) \ \& \ \text{Violent}(\eta)).$

(Here I follow the precedent of Chapter One, and abstract from the element of tense for the sake of clarity of the formalism. But of course that element could easily be restored by applying the methods of Chapter Three section 1.)

Logical relations obtaining between the unanalyzed (1)–(4) in virtue of adverbial elimination and commutation are preserved, we might note, amongst their paraphrases (1i)–(4i), being mediated by the properties of conjunction in just the way that they were in Davidson's own preferred paraphrases. The same properties also suffice in Davidson's case to account for the entailment by each of (1)–(4) of the simple

(5) Brutus stabbed Caesar.

That is not quite true of the paraphrases *MLE* recommends – from any of (1i)–(4i) the logic of conjunction will suffice to yield

(6) $(\exists\eta)(\exists t)(\eta = <\mathrm{Int}_{LE}(\text{'Stab'}),\mathrm{Brutus},\mathrm{Caesar},t>),$

but the natural paraphrase of (5) is not (6), but rather the simpler

(5i) $(\exists t)\mathrm{Stab}(\mathrm{Brutus},\mathrm{Caesar},t).$

Still, the entailments in question are accommodated, since (6) and (5i) are demonstrably equivalent under *nonlogical* principles of the theories of states of affairs and semantics *MLE* contains. (Specifically, the equivalence follows from the definitions of eventhood and obtaining, a modicum of set-theory, and a disquotational semantic principle governing *LE*'s primary model

$$\Delta\ (\mathrm{Int}_{LE}(\text{'Stab'})) = \{<x,y,t> | \mathrm{Stab}(x,y,t)\}.)$$

where 'Δ' is *MLE*'s device for mapping intensions onto extensions – *cf.* above, p. 40.)

2. All of which looks sufficiently encouraging to invite consideration of refinements. But before turning to that, I am compelled to consider a powerful objection put in conversation by Gareth Evans, which urges that the pattern of paraphrase the last section advocated will not really do. For, it contends, there is a range of perfectly possible cases, consistently describable in simple mode-adverbial terms, which resist coherent description in *MLE* under the technique of paraphrase adopted; and if this claim can be made out, it bodes extremely ill for the whole project of combining the present account of events with a Davidsonian view of mode-adverbs as event-predicates. Let us begin by looking in some detail at one such purportedly troublesome case.

Under our current proposal,

(7) Shem hit Shaun with a shillelagh violently

is rendered in *MLE* as

(7i) $(\exists\eta)(\exists t)(\eta = <\mathrm{Int}_{LE}(\text{'Hit'}),\mathrm{Shem},\mathrm{Shaun},t> \ \&$
       $(\exists z)(\mathrm{Shillelagh}(z) \ \& \ \mathrm{With}(z,\eta)) \ \& \ \mathrm{Violent}(\eta))$

and similarly

(8) Shem hit Shaun with a cudgel, but not violently

goes over as

(8i) $(\exists \eta)(\exists t)(\eta = <\text{Int}_{LE}(\text{'Hit'}),\text{Shem},\text{Shaun},t> \&$
     $(\exists z)(\text{Cudgel}(z) \& \text{With}(z,\eta)) \& \sim\text{Violent}(\eta)).$

But now – to construct the Evans case – suppose that a single time t_0 is a time of an ambidextrous battery of Shem upon Shaun performed both with shillelagh and with cudgel, and that the assault with the shillelagh is violently done though the cudgel-dealt blows are comparatively mild. Then both (7) and (8) become true, and true in virtue just of the goings-on at t_0. So (7i) and (8i) should also be true, and remain true when rendered more temporally specific by the addition of '$t = t_0$' to the matrix of each as an extra conjunct. But then *MLE*'s account of these perfectly consistent happenings is contradictory; for from (7i) and (8i) so augmented, elementary logic and set-theory are enough to derive

(9) $(\exists \eta)(\text{Violent}(\eta) \& \sim\text{Violent}(\eta)).$

The springs of this problem reside in the fact that my view of events evidently identifies Shem's shillelagh-wielding hitting at t_0 with his cudgel-dealt one, both being constructed as $<\text{Int}_{LE}(\text{'Hit'}),\text{Shem},\text{Shaun},t_0>$; which single event must by the Davidsonian treatment of adverbs absurdly fall both in and out of the extension of the predicate 'Violent'. A first reaction (Strategy One) to the case is accordingly to take Davidson's way with unwanted predications generated by event-identities which his own views license, and to rule 'violently' attributive, hence outside the range of straightforward application of the analysis (so that the troublesome (7i) and (8i) cease to be genuine renditions of (7) and (8)). This approach has its attraction, there being some pressure towards saying that, in the circumstances of t_0, Shem's hitting of Shaun was violent *qua* done-with-shillelagh though not *qua* done-with-cudgel, just as Mickey may be big *qua* mouse though not *qua* animal. Still, it looks *ad hoc*, since there is little independent motivation for taking 'violently' in its mode use as attributive. Further, by generalization of the example, the line seems likely to rule a host of other adverbs similarly attributive, robbing the main thesis of much interest. Finally, the view has difficulty in accounting for our evident willingness to apply adverbial commutation to (7) and infer

(10) Shem hit Shaun violently with a shillelagh

since attributiveness normally prohibits commutativity (expensive Taiwanese pianos need not be Taiwanese expensive pianos).

Another reaction (Strategy Two) is to deny that the 'with' of (7) and (8) functions as a preposition forming complex mode adverbs, and to rule that the verb 'hit' should properly be represented in *LE* not by a 3-place predicate 'Hit' as the foregoing has assumed but rather by a 4-place predicate 'Hit$^+$' whose extra argument-place is reserved for the instrument of hitting. (7) and (8) then get rendered into *MLE* not as the old (7i) and (8i), but rather as

$$(7\text{ii}) \ (\exists\eta)(\exists t)(\exists z)(\text{Shillelagh}(z) \ \&$$
$$\eta = <\text{Int}_{LE}(\text{'Hit}^+\text{'}),\text{Shem},\text{Shaun},z,t> \ \& \ \text{Violent}(\eta))$$

and

$$(8\text{ii}) \ (\exists\eta)(\exists t)(\exists z)(\text{Cudgel}(z) \ \&$$
$$\eta = <\text{Int}_{LE}(\text{'Hit}^+\text{'}),\text{Shem},\text{Shaun},z,t> \ \& \sim\text{Violent}(\eta)).$$

And these generate no problems, since, even in the *outré* circumstances of t_0, Shem's shillelagh-wielding hitting remains distinct from his hitting with a cudgel, each containing a distinct instrument as one constituent.

This second strategy is motivated by an intuition similar to its predecessor, that Shem's hitting of Shaun at t_0 was violent only *qua* done-with-a-shillelagh; but, by incorporating an instrument-place into the predicate, manages to formalize this intuition without having to pay the price of discounting 'violently' as non-standard. It suffers nevertheless from a number of drawbacks. First, one wonders how far this policy with instrumental 'with' is to go – if it is to be a universal one, the advantages of treating 'violently' as standard are offset by the need to single out 'with' for special treatment; if it is not, then there is the question of just when 'with' is to be viewed as a mode-adverb-forming preposition, and when by contrast it serves to mark an instrumental argument-place. Second, there is the problem of whether the 4-place 'Hit$^+$' is really suited

to represent 'hit' in contexts where no instrument is specified; presumably the idea must be to render the bare 'Shem
hit Shaun' as the doubly-quantified '$(\exists t)(\exists z)$ Hit$^+$(Shem,
Shaun,z,t)', but this ploy depends on the assumption that all
hitting involves some instrument (Of course, if Shem eschews a
weapon he still hits Shaun with something – *e.g.* a fist – in *some*
sense of 'with'. But it is not clear that this sense is the
instrumental one. The pure Davidsonian at least has a good
motive for saying that it is not; for, according to him, Oswald's
pulling the trigger (done with a finger) is the same event as
Oswald's killing Kennedy (done with a gun) – so he must say
that Oswald killed Kennedy with a finger and with a gun,
an oddity he will find it handy to dismiss as a zeugma.)
Third, Strategy Two like its predecessor has difficulty in
explaining how (7) comes to entail (10) by adverbial commutation – its line must be that both share a common form (7ii),
hence that the 'inference' is a matter of syntactic appearance
merely.

But these drawbacks to Strategy Two disappear if (Strategy
Three) we modify it to allow that 'hit' is ambiguous, being
representable in *LE* both by the 3-place 'Hit' and (in
appropriate contexts) by the 4-place 'Hit$^+$', and that the 'with'
of instrument is to be rendered sometimes prepositionally (via
the binary predicate 'With') and sometimes as the argument-
place of a predicate – as a marker in logical syntax of *case*.
Taking this view, 'Hit' and 'Hit$^+$' are construed as primitive
predicates of *LE*, logically independent but related intimately
nevertheless by a 'meaning-postulate' frameable in *MLE*,

(11) $\text{Hit}^+(x,y,z,t) \leftrightarrow (\exists\eta)(\eta = <\text{Int}_{LE}(\text{'Hit'}),x,y,t> \ \& $
$\text{With}(z,\eta))$

Treating 'with' as a marker of case or as a genuine preposition
are, given this postulate, equivalent in contexts involving no
further adverbial complication; but the lesson of the Evans
case is that this equivalence does not hold more generally.
More specifically, whilst it can always be counted true that

(12) $(\exists\eta)(\eta = <\text{Int}_{LE}(\text{'Hit'}),x,y,t> \ \& \ \text{With}(z,\eta) \ \& \ M(\eta))$
$\rightarrow .(\exists\eta_1)(\eta_1 = <\text{Int}_{LE}(\text{'Hit'}^+),x,y,z,t> \ \& \ M(\eta_1))$

(where 'M' schematically represents any event-predicate), the best that can be done by way of a universally-stated converse is more qualified:

$$(13)\ (\exists\eta_1)(\eta_1 = \,<\!\mathrm{Int}_{LE}(\text{'Hit}^+\text{'}),x,y,z,t\!> \ \&\ \mathrm{M}(\eta_1))$$
$$\&\ \sim(\exists z')(z \neq z' \ \&\ \mathrm{Hit}^+(x,y,z',t))$$
$$.\rightarrow.(\exists\eta)(\eta = \,<\!\mathrm{Int}_{LE}(\text{'Hit'}),x,y,t\!>$$
$$\&\ \mathrm{With}(z,\eta) \ \&\ \mathrm{M}(\eta)).$$

Applying this apparatus, we can evidently reap the advantages of Strategy Two without running foul of its disadvantages. The peculiarities of t_0 are accommodated at least to the extent that (7) and (8) have true and consistent renditions as (7ii) and (8ii). (They are renderable as well, of course, as (7i) and (8i), but the odd details of the case dictate that, as so construed, not both are true – nor need they be, given the way the meaning-postulates chart the relations between the various sentences in play.) (7) and (10) have one sense at least under which the former genuinely entails the latter. There is no need to construe the bare 'Shem hit Shaun' as containing a hidden quantification of a concealed argument-place for instrument – it is representable directly without such contrivances by means of the 3-place 'Hit'. And since the strategy allows that 'with' functions sometimes as a genuine preposition, it runs no risk of universally exempting 'with' from the range of the main analysis. (It does face the question of saying *when* it should be so exempted and treated rather as a mark of instrumental argument-place. An adequate answer perhaps is 'inasmuch as such construal is necessary to avoid Evans cases' – so that implementing Strategy Three provides a standard, not on general grounds entirely unwelcome, for measuring the logical complexity of primitive predicates.) The chief drawback of the approach is that, since (7i) and (8i) are contradictories in the context of t_0, it must in that context deem one true and the other false without providing any rationale for saying which is which. But this seems to be a defect a realist can live with.

3.   The Evans case just discussed has a generalizable structure: it is a case in which, in some time t, an agent x φ-ed M_1-ly M-ly but M_2-ly non M-ly. *Any* such case is going to raise problems for the mix of my favoured event-theory with Davidsonian

construal of mode adverbs as event-predicates, and a problem with the discussion of the last case is that there is no evident guarantee that its tactics will be adaptable to other examples.

In particular the last Evans case possessed a special feature, being one in which the 'M_1' and 'M_2' of the Evans-case schema were prepositional phrases, and Strategy Three may appear to have traded on the logical complexity thus introduced and local to the specific example. It is worth looking accordingly at an Evans case involving simple adverbs of mode only.

Suppose then that in some time t_1 a choir sang both highly melodiously and lowly non-melodiously. Then the pattern of reasoning familiar from the last case threatens once more; for we have both

(14) $(\exists \eta)(\exists t)(t = t_1$ & $\eta = <\text{Int}_{LE}(\text{'Sing'}),\text{the choir},t>$ & $\text{High}(\eta)$ & $\text{melodious}(\eta))$

and

(15) $(\exists \eta)(\exists t)(t = t_1$ & $\eta = <\text{Int}_{LE}(\text{'Sing'}),\text{the choir},t>$ & $\text{Low}(\eta)$ & $\sim\text{Melodious}(\eta))$

and can from these derive the contradictory

(16) $(\exists \eta)(\text{Melodious}(\eta)$ & $\sim\text{Melodious}(\eta))$.

Now, if any analogue of the previous manoeuvre is again to apply, the way to avoid commitment to this absurdity is going to be to find some means of consistently representing the facts of the case by invoking a predicate 'Sing^+' of *LE* with at least 3 places instead of the old 2-place 'Sing'; but whereas 'Hit^+' was constructed out of 'Hit' by, in effect, absorbing the preposition 'With' into the latter predicate, this time the case provides no handy absorbable preposition.[1]

Still, even if no 3-place 'Sing' emerges this time in just the way it did before, reflection on the nature of the informal 'sing'

[1] It might be suggested that the case be handled by using predicates 'Sing-highly' and 'Sing-lowly' (both dyadic like 'Sing' itself) formed by absorption of *adverbs* into the predicate. That would have some claim to being a procedure analogous to that employed in the previous case; but there seems no prospect of satisfactorily articulating the relations these predicates bear to each other and to 'Sing' itself, there being no analogue of (13) to bring into play.

shows such a predicate is available nevertheless; for 'sing' has a standard use as a transitive verb, in which it relates singer if not to song then at least to sound produced. And by construing the second argument-place of 'Sing$^+$' as marking this object of singing, the facts of t_1 can be accommodated by using, in place of the unsatisfactory (14) and (15),

> (14i) $(\exists\eta)(\exists t)(\exists y)(t = t_1$ & $\eta = <\mathrm{Int}_{LE}($'Sing$^+$'),the choir,$y,t>$ & High(η) & Melodious(η))

and

> (15i) $(\exists\eta)(\exists t)(\exists y)(t = t_1$ & $\eta = <\mathrm{Int}_{LE}($'Sing$^+$'),the choir,$y,t>$ & Low(η) & ~Melodious(η))

with no fear of contradiction arising. And if – though the motivation this time seems less strong – it is deemed desirable that the old 2-place 'Sing' should survive in *LE* beside its 3-place sister, the two can be linked in *MLE* by an analogue of (11), introducing the special preposition 'Of' for the purpose:

> (17) Sing$^+$$(x,y,t)$ ↔ $(\exists\eta)(\eta = <\mathrm{Int}_{LE}($'Sing'),$x,t>$ & Of(y,η).

And further relations between the two can be charted by obvious analogues of (12) and (13).

If the treatment just meted out to this second Evans case is not a precise analogue to that accorded to the first, the matter is of little consequence; for Evans cases, despite their common structure, depend for their plausibility on the details of the verbal and adverbial structures they contain, and the proper way with them is to pay due attention to those details. Constructing Evans cases invites complexity, and purported examples can sometimes be dismissed as not genuinely intelligible, or as intelligible only when contained adverbs are assigned a non-mode reading. Other cases involve adverbial constructions which are plausibly regarded on independent grounds as attributive, and so can be dealt with by the Strategy One dismissed in application to the first example. For the residue, there is the 'expanding argument-place' tactic in one of the two versions we have applied it to the two cases discussed. By judicious application of manoeuvres like these to the various cases arising, I think we can turn the force of Evans' awkward objection.

4.   It seems accordingly that the current explication of events can be made to blend with a Davidsonian construal of mode adverbs as event-predicates at least to the extent of permitting acceptable paraphrases of simple adverbial sentences into the language *MLE* of the explication. But how do we fare with the nuances of adverbial modification?

Chapter One observed one such nuance – that mode adverbs do not happily tolerate negated verbs inside their scope, so that a decent story of the way they operate should account for the deficiency of *e.g.* the old example

(18)   Brutus violently did not stab Caesar.

And this it seems *MLE* is able to do. For while it is true that (18) receives a perfectly well-formed paraphrase in *MLE*, going over as

(18i) $(\exists \eta)(\exists t)(\eta = <\sim,<\text{Int}_{LE}(\text{'Stab'}),\text{Brutus},\text{Caesar},t>>$
          & Violent(η)),

the theory of events *MLE* incorporates deems that paraphrase *a priori* false, by ruling out the possibility of the existence of an event of the sort (18i) requires (see above, p. 89). Davidson's own theory apparently accounted for (18)'s deviance by refusing to supply it a coherent paraphrase at all; but it was urged above (p. 25) that such a treatment was open to a charge of arbitrariness, and required underpinning by a negative ontological thesis to justify its restrictions. *MLE* supplies the thesis required, and diagnoses (18)'s deficiences by appealing to it directly.

A second adverbial subtlety Chapter One noted was the ambiguity mode-adverbs can generate when combined with quantifiers, as exemplified in

(19)   Henry gracefully ate all the crisps.

In the sense (19a) in which (19) asserts graceful eating of each individual crisp, it evidently goes over into *MLE* straight-forwardly as

(19ai) $(\forall x)(\text{Crisp}(x) \rightarrow (\exists \eta)(\exists t)(\eta =$
           $<\text{Int}_{LE}(\text{'Eat'}),\text{Henry},x,t> \ \& \ \text{Graceful}(\eta)))$.

It is less clear how we should handle it in sense (19b), when it is compatible with graceless devoural of the odd crisp.

Evidently, the idea must be to construe (19) in sense (19b) as asserting gracefulness of an event formed by summing all of Henry's individual crisp-eatings. Assuming 'Eat' to be a K-predicate meeting Chapter Three's Postulate 7, and that Henry's individual crisp-eatings manifest an appropriate temporal continuity, it is true too that the present explication provides for the existence of the appropriate event-sum, identifying it with the set containing as members $<\mathrm{Int}_{LE}($'Eat'$)$, Henry,$x,t>$ for each crisp x, where t is the time stretching from the lower bound of Henry's starting on his first crisp through to the upper bound of his swallowing the last. What remains to be seen is how we can make *MLE* talk appropriately of this event-sum.

The event of which we wish to speak is a special one; in the terminology of the last chapter's [D1] (p. 86) it is an event which is also *primarily* eventlike. That is, it is what we might call a *primary event*: an event which is a set containing as members only atomic states of affairs. Let us use 'η^*', 'η_1^*', etc. as variables of *MLE* over such primary events. Then the event of which we wish to speak is a primary one containing as elements for the appropriate t, all and only atomic states of affairs $<\mathrm{Int}_{LE}($'Eat'$)$,Henry,$x,t>$ where x is a crisp. So it seems the way to render (19) in its second sense into *MLE* is as

(19bi) $(\exists\eta^*)(\exists t)((\forall\xi)(\xi\in\eta^* \leftrightarrow (\exists x)(\mathrm{Crisp}(x)\ \&$
$\xi = <\mathrm{Int}_{LE}($'Eat'$)$,Henry,$x,t>))\ \&\ \mathrm{Graceful}(\eta^*))$.

Which does indeed say what we want it to. But it says it with little elegance, and it is hard to rest content with a diagnosis of the ambiguity of (19) via paraphrases like (19ai) and (19bi) which are too divergent to be of much use in pinpointing the locus of the ambivalence. It is accordingly worth investigating the claims of a new method of paraphrase into *MLE*, which promises to furnish representations in *MLE* of adverbial sentences equivalent to the old paraphrases, but in a form which more illuminates the vagaries of (19).

5. Every event is, under the favoured explication, equivalent to a primary one. So if mode-adverbs are event-predicates, every adverbial statement should be equivalent to a statement about primary events only – or, at least, that should be true if

the event-predicates by which *MLE* represents mode adverbs are closed under the equivalence of events, so that we have for each such predicate P^n,

$$[\text{I}] \quad \eta \overset{LE}{\approx} \eta' \rightarrow (P^n(x_1 \ldots x_{n-1}, \eta) \leftrightarrow P^n(x_1 \ldots x_{n-1}, \eta'))$$

The essence of the new method of paraphrase is to find the primary-event-equivalents of the old paraphrases which, this thought suggests, must be there to be found, and then to utilize definition to bring the equivalents once found into perspicuous order.

Any primary event of *LE* is a set of *LE*'s atomic states of affairs; and by the definition of p. 86, these constituent atomic states share a common predicative element. So we can in *MLE* define a primary event as a *stabbing* if the common predicative element is the intension of *LE*'s 'Stab', as a *running* if it is the intension of *LE*'s 'Run', and so on; that is, we define in *MLE*

[Def 1] (a) η^* is a *stabbing* $\leftrightarrow$ $(\forall \xi) \xi \in \eta^* \rightarrow$
$\quad (\exists x)(\exists y)(\exists t)(\xi = <\text{Int}_{LE}(\text{'Stab'}),x,y,t>))$

(b) η^* is a *running* $\leftrightarrow$ $(\forall \xi)(\xi \in \eta^* \rightarrow$
$\quad (\exists x)(\exists t)(\eta = <\text{Int}_{LE}(\text{'Run'}),x,t>)),$

continuing the list to the exhaustion of *LE*'s primitive K- and E-predicates. The definition of a primary event ensures moreover that all such an event's components share a common temporal element, and we can specify the time *occupied by* a primary event as being that common element:

[Def 2] η^* *occupies* t $\leftrightarrow$ $(\exists P^n)(\forall \xi)(\xi \in \eta^* \rightarrow$
$\quad (\exists x_1) \ldots (\exists x_{n+1})(\xi = <\text{Int}_{LE}(P^n),x_1 \ldots x_{n-1},t>)).$

Components of primary events can diverge in elements beyond the predicative and the temporal just singled out, but this need not prevent us from introducing terminology to describe the relation between a primary event and these more divergent elements of its components. In particular we might describe a primary event which is a running as being 'by'[2]

---

[2] This 'by', derived as it is from *LE*'s grammar, is not meant to mark the full-blooded 'by' of agency. It should accordingly be construed as a purely formal device, though one which is not perhaps totally unreflected in surface English – for in some formal sense at least we are happy to say that a tripping was done 'by' Jan if she tripped, even when we know that trip was accidental and hence attribute to her no agency in the matter.

Socrates if it contains some component $<\text{Int}_{LE}(\text{'Run'}),x,t>$ whose first nonpredicative element x is Socrates; a primary stabbing as being *by* Brutus if it contains some component $<\text{Int}_{LE}(\text{'Stab'}),x,y,t>$ whose first nonpredicative component x is Brutus; and more generally define

[Def 3] η^* is *by* $x \leftrightarrow (\exists\xi)(\xi \in \eta^* \ \& \ (\exists P^{n\geqslant 2})(\exists x_1) \ldots$
$(\exists x_{n-1})(\exists t)(\xi = <\text{Int}_{LE}(P^n),x_1 \ldots x_{n-1},t>$
$\& \ x_1 = x))$.

And in similar vein, we can describe a primary defeat as being '*of*'[3] Capablanca just in case it has a component $<\text{Int}_{LE}$ ('Defeat'),$x,y,t>$ whose *second* nonpredicative component y is Capablanca, and define in general

[Def 4] η^* is *of* $x \leftrightarrow (\exists\xi)(\xi \in \eta^* \ \&$
$(\exists P^{n\geqslant 3})(\exists x_1) \ldots (\exists x_{n-1})(\exists t)(\xi =$
$<\text{Int}_{LE}(P^n),x_1 \ldots x_{n-1},t> \ \& \ x_2 = x))$.

And note that, though 'by' and 'of' are all that examples in the sequel will require, this definitional process could in principle continue, with arbitrarily-invented defined predicates, until we had reached the uppermost nonpredicative component which *LE*, with its finite stock of primitive predicates, allows any atomic state of affairs to have.

Resurrecting now an old abbreviatory pattern from Chapter One (p. 18), observe that

η^* is by x uniquely

comes to mean

η^* is by x & $(\forall y)(\eta^*$ is by $y \rightarrow y = x)$

and hence, by [Def 3], that η^* has only components having x as first nonpredicative element. A similar point holding for 'of', it follows that *e.g.*

η^* is a stabbing & η^* is by x uniquely & η^* is of y uniquely & η^* occupies t

---

[3] This predicate 'is of' must be distinguishable from the 'Of' introduced in the last section (see (17), p. 105). Where $\text{Sing}^+(x,y,t)$, we have $\text{Of}(y,$ $<\text{Int}_{LE}(\text{'Sing'}),x,t,>)$, but not, of course, that $<\text{Int}_{LE}(\text{'Sing'}),x,t>$ is of y; though what is true along the latter lines is that $\{<\text{Int}_{LE}(\text{'Sing}^+\text{'}),x,y,t>\}$ is of y.

means that η^* has $<\mathrm{Int}_{LE}(\text{'Stab'}),x,y,t>$ as sole component, *i.e.* that $\eta^* = \{<\mathrm{Int}_{LE}(\text{'Stab'}),x,y,t>\}$. Which gives the clue for turning old style paraphrases of adverbial sentences which prattle of events generally into new-style ones which speak, in abbreviated form, of primary events only.

Take for example, the paradigm example

(1)   Brutus stabbed Caesar violently.

Old style paraphrase into *MLE* rendered this as

(1i) $(\exists\eta)(\exists t)(\eta = <\mathrm{Int}_{LE}(\text{'Stab'}),\mathrm{Brutus,Caesar},t> \&$
       $\mathrm{Violent}(\eta))$.

This in turn is equivalent in *MLE* to

(1i′) $(\exists\eta)(\exists t)(\eta = \{<\mathrm{Int}_{LE}(\text{'Stab'}),\mathrm{Brutus,Caesar},t>\} \&$
       $\mathrm{Violent}(\eta))$

given the assumption [I] of p. 108, that *MLE*'s event-predicates are closed under event-equivalence; for by the key definition of p. 45, $\xi \overset{LE}{\approx} \{\xi\}$ quite generally. But to speak of $\{<\mathrm{Int}_{LE}(\text{'Stab'}),$ $\mathrm{Brutus,Caesar},t>\}$ is, as just noted, to speak of an η^* which is a stabbing, by Brutus uniquely, of Caesar uniquely, and occupying t; so (1i′), and with it (1i), are equivalent in *MLE* to

(1ii) $(\exists\eta^*)(\exists t)(\eta^*$ is a stabbing & η^* is by Brutus
        uniquely & η^* is of Caesar uniquely & η^* occupies t
        & $\mathrm{Violent}(\eta^*))$.

The pattern thus displayed will clearly work to generate equivalent new-style paraphrases for all the simpler cases of adverbial sentences with which we have dealt. As for Henry's crisp-eating, (19) in its sense (a) in which it requires graceful eating of each crisp goes over, by the same pattern, as

(19aii) $(\forall x)(\mathrm{Crisp}(x) \rightarrow (\exists\eta^*)(\exists t)(\eta^*$ is an eating
          & η^* is by Henry uniquely & η^* is of x
          uniquely & η^* occupies t & $\mathrm{Graceful}(\eta^*)))$,

an equivalent in *MLE* of the old (19ai); whereas in the alternative sense it can be rendered as

(19bii) $(\exists\eta^*(\exists t)(\eta^*$ is an eating & η^* is by Henry uniquely
          & $(\forall x)(\eta^*$ is of $x \leftrightarrow \mathrm{Crisp}(x))$ & η^* occupies t
          & $\mathrm{Graceful}(\eta^*))$,

an equivalent of the old (19bi). And I find this new-style way of displaying (19)'s ambiguity sufficiently elegant to opt from now on for new-style paraphrases of adverbial sentences as the official renditions into *MLE*, regarding the equivalent but clumsier old-style of paraphrase as a cast-away ladder towards the new way's improved perspective.

6. But paraphrase into *MLE*, however elegant, is hardly to the point when our aim is to forge a theory of sense for mode-adverbial English sentences adequate by Chapter One's lights. True, *MLE* is in structure standardly first-order, and there is accordingly no bar to applying Tarski's methods to it next to obtain an austerely adequate truth-theory. But the T-sentences the resulting theory generates will state truth-conditions for *MLE* sentences using the concepts those sentences themselves deploy, and these are both unabashedly metalinguistic and heavily set-theoretic (even if the latter feature is disguised in new-style paraphrases by the use of abbreviating definitions). So to treat *MLE* paraphrases as *base* paraphrases, and to construe its Tarskian truth-theory as a theory of sense, is to attribute metalinguistic and set-theoretic content to everyday utterances of even the simplest mode-adverbial English sentences. Which won't do.

It does not however follow that the whole exercise of paraphrasing into *MLE* is totally futile, or that it provides no clue to the form genuine base paraphrases should assume. The situation is analogous to that which arises when we render a numerical statement like

(20)   One is less than three

into a formal set-theory such as ZF, obtaining (under the von Neumann analysis)

(20i) $\{\emptyset\} \in \{\emptyset\{\emptyset\}, \{\emptyset,\{\emptyset\}\}\}$

or some definitional contraction thereof. Again, this won't do as a base paraphrase for the informal (20), since its set-theoretic ideology will carry over into the content-ascriptions generated by its truth-theory regarded as a theory of sense. Instead we should favour as a *base* paraphrase for (20) a rendering into a language of formal number theory as

(20ii) succ(0) $<$ succ(succ(succ(0)))

(where 'succ' is the successor functor), or some definitional contraction thereof; a paraphrase which naively accepts (20)'s numerical commitment and is happy merely to display its content in a form adequate for the systematic ends of axiomatics and of truth-theory. Still, (20i) and (20ii) are not unconnected – the set-theoretic paraphrase *explicates* the number-theoretic one, explaining notions which number-theory accepts as primitive in its own more fundamental terms (thus, analyzing '$<$' as '$\in$', '0' as '$\emptyset$', and 'succ(n)' as '$n \cup \{n\}$'). By analogy, then, we should seek for base paraphrases of adverbial sentences as ones which utilize a naive apparatus of events and states of affairs, and which the precise *MLE* renditions can be regarded as explicating.

I suggest that paraphrases of the desired sort are forthcoming in an extension LE^+ of LE, formed by augmenting LE with an apparatus sufficient for it naively to discuss its own events and its own states of affairs more generally. First, let us add to LE an operator 'ST' (read 'the state of affairs that'), capable of combining syntactically with a sentence of LE to form a singular term (or 'state expression') denoting the state of affairs that sentence describes, so that

[FR1] If A is a wff of LE, ST[A] is a term of LE^+.

In addition, let us supply LE^+ with variables 'X', 'Y', 'Z', 'X_1', 'Y_1', 'Z_1', . . . ranging over states of affairs posited by LE. Call these 'state variables' of LE^+; and group them with the state expressions to form the *second-level terms* of LE^+, its first-level terms being just the terms of LE unaugmented.

Further, LE^+ is going to need a range of *second-level predicates*, predicates in addition to the first-level ones present already in LE. These new predicates I envisage as coming in various *types*, where a type for an n-place second-level predicate is an n-long sequence $<i_1 \ldots i_n>$, where each $i_j = 1$ or $= 2$, and the fact that the j-th place of a predicate's type is 1 or 2 reflects a requirement that that predicate requires a term of corresponding level in its j-th place for well-formedness to be achieved. Specifically, LE^+ should contain second-level predicates of appropriate types, corresponding to the various

event predicates added to *MLE* to regiment mode adverbs –
thus, *e.g.*, predicates 'GRACEFUL' and 'VIOLENT' (both of
type $<2>$) corresponding to *MLE*'s 'Graceful' and 'Violent' in
their application to primary events, and a predicate 'WITH' of
type $<2,1>$ corresponding to *MLE*'s 'With' in similar application. And over and above these, LE^+ needs a second-level
identity predicate '$=$' of type $<2,2>$ to put beside the equiform
first-level identity predicate *LE* already contains, and also
primitive second-level predicates corresponding to (sometimes
defined) *MLE* predicates of the theory of states of affairs: a
predicate 'Ob' of type $<2>$ (read as 'obtains', and corresponding to *MLE*'s 'obtains$_{LE}$'), a predicate 'Ev' of type $<2>$ (read as
'is an event', but representing more specifically *MLE*'s 'is a
primary event$_{LE}$'), and a predicate 'Cons' of type $<2,2>$ (read
'is a constituent of', and representing *MLE's* '$\in$' when it relates
states of affairs to more complex ones which contain them).
Obvious formation-rules then serve to generate the well-
formed formulae of LE^+:

[FR2] Any wff of *LE* is a first-level wff of LE^+;

[FR3] If P^n is a second-level predicate of LE^+ of
        type $<i_1 \ldots i_n>$ and, for each j from 1 to n, t_j is
        a term of level i_j, $P^n t_1 \ldots t_n$ is an atomic second-
        level wff of LE^+.

[FR4] If A is a wff of LE^+ of second level, so is $\sim$A.

[FR5] If A and B are wffs of LE^+ at least one of which is of
        second-level, (A&B) is a second-level wff of LE^+.

[FR6] If A is a second-level wff of LE^+, so are $(\forall v_i)$A
        and $(\forall V_i)$A (where v_i and V_i are, respectively,
        the *i*-th ordinary and the *i*-th state variable of LE^+).

We can now proceed to introduce into LE^+ some defined
terminology, mimicking in LE^+'s naive terms the definitions
[Def 1]–[Def 4] which got the new-style analysis of adverbial
sentences into *MLE* under way. [Def 1] has an obvious enough
analogue:

[Def 1'] (a) X is a STABBING $\leftrightarrow$
$\qquad$ $Ev(X)$ & $(\forall Y)(Cons(Y,X) \rightarrow$
$\qquad$ $(\exists x)(\exists y)(\exists t)(Y = ST[Stab(x,y,t)]))$
$\qquad$ (b) X is a RUNNING $\leftrightarrow$
$\qquad$ $Ev(X)$ & $(\forall Y)(Cons(Y,X) \rightarrow$
$\qquad$ $(\exists x)(\exists t)(Y = ST[Run(x,t)]))$

where the clauses continue once more till LE's K- and E-predicates are exhausted. As for [Def 2]–[Def 4], they too find analogues in LE^+ provided we allow ourselves to use the existential quantifier, substitutionally interpreted, in combination with substitutional variables φ^n taking as their substituends n-place primitive K- and E-predicates of LE. For then we can write

[Def 2'] X OCCUPIES $t \leftrightarrow$
$\qquad$ $Ev(X)$ & $(\exists \varphi^n)(\forall Y)(Cons(Y,X) \rightarrow$
$\qquad$ $(\exists x_1) \ldots (\exists x_{n-1})(\exists t)(Y =$
$\qquad$ $ST[\varphi^n, x_1 \ldots x_{n-1}, t]))$

[Def 3'] X is BY $x \leftrightarrow$
$\qquad$ $Ev(X)$ & $(\exists Y)(Cons(Y,X)$ &
$\qquad$ $(\exists \varphi^{n \geq 2})(\exists x_1) \ldots (\exists x_{n-1})(\exists t)(Y =$
$\qquad$ $ST[\varphi^n(x_1 \ldots x_{n-1}, t)]$ & $x_1 = x))$

[Def 4'] X is OF $x \leftrightarrow$
$\qquad$ $Ev(X)$ & $(\exists Y)(Cons(Y,X)$ &
$\qquad$ $(\exists \varphi^{n \geq 3})(\exists x_1) \ldots (\exists x_{n-1})(\exists t)(Y =$
$\qquad$ $ST[\varphi^n(x_1 \ldots x_{n-1}, t)]$ & $x_2 = x))$

and note that the series which the definitions of 'BY' and 'OF' begin could once again in principle be extended, with made-up defined predicates, to embrace the uppermost limit of the degrees of LE's primitive K- and E-predicates. And finally, we observe that the definitions [Def 2']–[Def 4'] just given can be allowed to stand as genuine definitions within LE^+. For the device of substitutional quantification over LE's primitive K-

and E-predicates which was needed to frame them is not really as extraneous to LE^+ as may have appeared, since – given the finite number of the primitive predicates in the substitution class – its force can be reconstructed within LE^+ proper by construing a quantification of the form

$$(\exists\varphi^n)A$$

as an abbreviation for the finite disjunction[4]

$$A(P^n_1/\varphi^n) \lor A(P^n_2/\varphi^n) \lor \ldots \lor A(P^n_m/\varphi^n)$$

where $P^n_1, \ldots, P^n_m$ exhaust LE's n-place K- and E-predicates.

With this much apparatus in hand, it is now child's play to render mode-adverbial sentences into LE^+ in a way reflecting the structure of the new-style paraphrases into MLE previously canvassed. Thus, the old 'Brutus stabbed Caesar violently', going over into MLE as

(1ii) $(\exists\eta^*)(\exists t)(\eta^*$ is a stabbing & η^* is by Brutus uniquely & η^* is of Caesar uniquely & η^* occupies t & Violent(η^*))

can be rendered in LE^+ as

(1iii) $(\exists X)(\exists t)($Ev(X) & X is a STABBING & X is BY Brutus uniquely & X is OF Caesar uniquely & X OCCUPIES t & VIOLENT$(X))$

whilst in analogous fashion the case of Henry and the crisps will be dealt with in LE^+ by assigning (19) the two paraphrases

(19aiii) $(\forall x)($Crisp$(x) \rightarrow (\exists X)(\exists t)(Ev(X)$ & X is an EATING & X is BY Henry uniquely & X is OF x uniquely & X OCCUPIES t & GRACEFUL$(X)))$

---

[4] Here, of course, '$A(P/\varphi)$' is the result of replacing all free occurrences of φ in A by P; similarly for the notation '$A(t/t')$' which will occur in the sequel, which is the result of replacing all free occurrences of t' in A by t. (Contrast the notation '$A(t//t')$' of Chapter Two, which marks the result of replacing *some* occurrences only of t' in A by t).

and

(19biii) $(\exists X)(\exists t)(\text{Ev}(X)$ & X is an EATING & X is BY
Henry uniquely & $(\forall x)(X$ is OF $x \leftrightarrow \text{Crisp}(x))$
& X OCCUPIES t & GRACEFUL$(X))$

corresponding to the *MLE* paraphrases (19aii) and (19bii). And
these paraphrases in LE^+ look like good candidates for the sort
of thing we earlier thought base paraphrases for mode
adverbial sentences might be: paraphrases which deploy the
apparatus of events and states of affairs naively, and which the
more sophisticated corresponding paraphrases in *MLE* explicate. In fact, we can be quite precise about the sort of
explication involved – see this Chapter's Postscript.

One might incidentally wonder whether LE^+, conceptually
austere though it may appear in comparison with *MLE*, is yet
not over-supplied with resources. For the LE^+ treatment of
mode-adverbial sentences just sketched nowhere appeals to a
state-term 'ST[A]' where A is more than atomic, and one might
accordingly question the need for allowing complex wffs into
the matrix of such terms. Recall, however, that a decision was
made back in section 5 of the last chapter (p. 90) to treat
causation as a relation between facts; which suggests that a
sentence like

(21) The dog's not barking caused Holmes's suspicion

should go over into *MLE* in some such fashion as

(21i) $(\exists \xi)(\exists t)(\xi = <\sim, <\text{Int}_{LE}(\text{'Bark'}),\text{the dog},t>>$
& $(\exists \zeta)(\exists t')(\zeta = <\text{Int}_{LE}(\text{'Suspicious'}),\text{Holmes},t'>$
& ξ obtains$_{LE}$ & ζ obtains$_{LE}$ & Cause$(\xi,\zeta)))$.

And to render this into LE^+ (suitably augmented with its own
causation predicate) as

(21ii) $(\exists X)(\exists t)(X = \text{ST}[\sim\text{Bark}(\text{the dog},t)]$ &
$(\exists Y)(\exists t')(Y = \text{ST}[\text{Suspicious}(\text{Holmes},t')]$ & Ob(X)
& Ob(Y) & CAUSE$(X,Y)))$

a complex formula must be admitted into the matrix of a state
term. Consideration of further sentences such as

(22) Everything's being quiet caused Watson's immobility

provides further support for thinking causal sentences, if not adverbial ones themselves, are going to need the full force of LE^+'s 'ST'.

7. Paraphrase into MLE preserves intuitive entailments of mode-adverbial sentences, inasmuch as the machinery of the theory of states of affairs which MLE incorporates suffices to generate paraphrases of entailed sentences from paraphrases of entailing ones. That mediating machinery, however, utilizes MLE's set-theoretic articulation of key concepts, and its role will need to be supplanted in LE^+ by axiomatic adoption of parallel principles cast in LE^+'s own more meagre terms. It is a test of the adequacy of LE^+ that it should reveal sufficient structure in adverbial sentences to enable the necessary proof-theoretic principles to be stated. Not that there is any need to go overboard on the matter, and attempt to supply LE^+ with a proof-theory capable of performing every inferential trick of which the theory embedded in MLE is capable; we can happily admit that some of the more subtle links between LE^+ sentences emerge only when their content is properly explicated in MLE. Still, we should expect at least to be able to articulate in LE^+ the grosser logical relations between the adverbial sentences it claims to represent. Foremost amongst these are entailments by adverbial commutation and elimination, upon which we shall accordingly concentrate.

Where an inference of such a kind leads to a conclusion which is itself adverbially modified, the structure of LE^+ paraphrase is such that it need rely on no more than logic, in particular the properties of conjunction, to justify the entailment; no more than this is required, for example, to move from the LE^+ paraphrase of 'Brutus stabbed Caesar violently with a knife' to its versions of such entailed sentences as 'Brutus stabbed Caesar with a knife violently', 'Brutus stabbed Caesar violently', or 'Brutus stabbed Caesar with a knife'. Where things get stickier is at the point where we move by adverbial elimination from 'Brutus stabbed Caesar violently' to the nonadverbial 'Brutus stabbed Caesar' or, as LE^+ puts it, from (liii) to

(23) $(\exists t)$Stab(Brutus,Caesar,t).

A problem with the same entailment was observed to arise for *MLE* back in the first section of this chapter, and to be there solved by theses of the theory of states of affairs *MLE* incorporates. LE^+ needs its own proof-theoretic principle to bridge the same gap.

But the requisite principles are not far to seek. For from LE^+'s version (1iii) of 'Brutus stabbed Caesar violently', we can derive quickly enough, appealing just to predicate logic with identity and to the definitions [Def 1']–[Def 4'], that there is a time t_1 and an X_1 such that

(24) $Ev(X_1)$ & $(\exists Y)(Cons(Y,X_1)$ &
$Y = ST[Stab(Brutus,Caesar,t_1)])$.

Assuming then as principles of LE^+

[AX 1] $Ev(X) \rightarrow Ob(X)$
[AX 2] $(\exists Y)Cons(Y,X) \rightarrow$
$(Ob(X) \leftrightarrow (\forall Z)(Cons(Z,X) \rightarrow Ob(Z)))$

we can derive from (24) that

(25) $Ob(ST[Stab(Brutus,Caesar,t_1)])$.

To move further, we need further to supply LE^+ with the *Axioms of Obtaining*, providing, for each primitive predicate P^n of *LE*, an instance of the schema

[AX OB 1] $Ob(ST[P^n x_1 \ldots x_n]) \leftrightarrow P^n x_1 \ldots x_n$

and in addition laying down as axioms all instances of the schemata

[AX OB 2] $Ob(ST[{\sim}A]) \leftrightarrow {\sim}Ob(ST[A])$
[AX OB 3] $Ob(ST[A\&B]) \leftrightarrow Ob(ST[A])$ & $Ob(ST[B])$
[AX OB 4] $Ob(ST[\forall v_i)A] \leftrightarrow (\forall v_i) Ob(ST[A])$.

For then from (25) we can derive that $Stab(Brutus,Caesar,t_1)$, thus validating the inference from (1iii) to (23).

Notice that the proof-theoretic principles which achieve this happy result are all ones which are valid on our explication of the concepts involved, insofar as each is explicated in *MLE* by a thesis of the theory of events and states of affairs that language embeds. Observe too that the same principles will serve to derive 'Henry ate all the crisps' from 'Henry gracefully ate all the crisps' in either of the two senses (19aiii) and (19biii) which LE^+ bestows on that ambiguous sentence. Indeed, to validate any of these entailments of adverbial sentences we can get by using just appropriate instances of [AX OB 1]; the later schematic Axioms of Obtaining come into their own only when we turn beyond adverbial sentences to causal ones, seeking e.g. to account for the inference of 'The dog did not bark' from 'The dog's not barking caused Holmes's suspicion'.

8. *MLE* paraphrases were excluded from candidature as base paraphrases by being fraught with a conceptual load which a Tarskian truth-theory will carry with it into its assignments of truth-conditions to the paraphrasing sentences, disqualifying it by Chapter One's lights from legitimate construal as a theory of sense for the adverbial sentences *MLE* paraphrases. LE^+ renderings shed a good deal of *MLE*'s conceptual freight, by unashamedly naive deployment of concepts from the theory of events and of states of affairs which *MLE* goes to the trouble to define, at the ideological cost we have lately found so objectionable. But if LE^+ renderings promise by their conceptual simplicity to provide the basis for the theory of truth construable as a theory of sense which we seek, it remains to be shown that they actually do. For LE^+ is not standardly first-order, so that we cannot rely on Tarskian methods alone to provide a theory of truth stating the truth-conditions for its sentences in their own suitably naive terms. We had better then establish that some extension of those methods will turn the trick, or else face the spectre that there is no truth-theory for LE^+ which does not resurrect in the apparatus it requires the very conceptual complexity we have attempted to shed, thereby disqualifying LE^+-paraphrases too, whatever their initial promise, from legitimate construal as base paraphrases.

Given purely first-order L, Tarski showed us how to construct a theory of truth for L adequate by his Convention T (and hence, by the current lights, adequate as a theory of sense for L) in a language $L*$ containing just (a) L itself, or some first-order-language into which L's sentences are, in Tarski's rather restricted sense, translatable; (b) number-theory; (c) the theory of sequences having as elements the items of which L speaks;

(d) primitive[5] semantic apparatus, specifically the satisfaction predicate for L 's Sat_L A' (read 'sequence s satisfies formula A in L') and the sequence-relative denotation functor 'den_L (t,s)' (read 'the denotation in L of term t relative to sequence s'); and (e) the theory of L's syntax, this last being theoretically dispensable in view of (b) and the possibility of the arithmetization of syntax. We may take as our last challenge, accordingly, that of providing a way of constructing a truth-theory for LE^+ in a language $[LE^+]^*$ with similar resources; and for concreteness and without loss of generality, concentrate on the 'homophonic' case in which $[LE^+]^*$ meets condition (a) by containing LE^+ itself.

Of course, LE^+ is *largely* if not entirely first-order, and we can draw upon Tarskian methods to accommodate its first-order fragment. Indeed, upon scrutiny it appears that LE^+ diverges from absolute first-orderhood in two respects only: its variables divide into two levels, and it contains state-terms 'ST[A]' formed by means of the non-first-order 'ST' (all other syntactic quirks of LE^+ being consequent on these two). As to the first divergence, Tarski himself ('Concept of Truth', p. 227 and following) pointed to the generalization of his method which will accommodate it – the sequences to which the key semantic concepts of denotation and satisfaction are relativized should be regarded as two-rowed, with ordinary variables drawing their values from the upper, state-variables from the lower, of the two rows distinguished.

Which accordingly leaves as the only unanswered question that of how a truth-theory cast in $[LE^+]^*$ should deal with the state-terms of LE^+. To what does that amount? Recall that we settled recently to aim for a homophonic truth-theory, *i.e.* for one generating instances of the 'disquotational' schema

(II) $T(A) \leftrightarrow A$

whenever A is a closed formula of LE^+. (I depart here from my previous pedantry, and drop the subscript 'LE^+' from the truth-predicate 'T' in the interests of both printer and reader;

---

[5] Tarski envisages eliminating the need for treating these as primitive by adding sufficient set-theory to L^* and then using a formal ruse of Frege's. But I ignore this twist as beside the point of the present enterprise.

similarly for the semantic vocabulary 'Sat' and 'den' to follow.) Within the context of Tarskian truth-theory, to generate instances of [II] it will suffice to generate similar disquotational instances of the satisfaction-schema[6]

$$\text{(III)} \quad \text{Sat}(A,s) \leftrightarrow A(\text{den}(v_{i_1},s)/v_{i_1}, \ldots, \text{den}(v_{i_k},s)/v_{i_k})$$

where A is any wff of LE^+ and $v_{i_1} \ldots v_{i_k}$ exhaust the free variables of A. And that in turn demands that *terms* of LE^+ are similarly assigned sequence-relative denotations by the theory in the disquotational mode, *i.e.* that the theory generates all instances of

$$\text{(IV)} \quad \text{den}(t,s) = t(\text{den}(v_{i_1},s)/v_{i_1}, \ldots, \text{den}(v_{i_k},s)/v_{i_k}))$$

where t is a term of LE^+ whose free variables $v_{i_1} \ldots v_{i_k}$ exhaust. Our final unsettled question of 'dealing with' the state-terms of LE^+ reduces accordingly to that of producing axioms adequate to generate the relevant instances of [IV] – adequate, that is, to generate all instances of

$$[\text{IV}'] \quad \text{den}(\text{ST}[A],s) = \text{ST}[A(\text{den}(v_{i_1},s)/v_{i_1}, \ldots,$$
$$\text{den}(v_{i_k},s)/v_{i_k})]$$

where A is a wff of LE and $v_{i_1} \ldots v_{i_k}$ exhaust its free variables.

And this it seems easy enough to do, provided we are prepared to equip the language $[LE^+]^*$ in which the theory is to be cast with a rich enough proof-theory and a modicum of additional apparatus. We begin by covering atomic state-terms in the obvious way, making, for each primitive first-level predicate P^n of LE^+, a stipulation of the form

$$[\text{den 1}] \quad \text{den}(\text{ST}[P^n t_1 \ldots t_n],s)$$
$$= \text{ST}[P^n \text{den}(t_1,s) \ldots \text{den}(t_n,s)]$$

Turning next to negated sentences, we suppose $[LE^+]^*$ to contain a unary functor 'NEG' of second level and type $<2>$, so functioning as to validate all instances of the schema

$$[\text{AX NEG}] \quad \text{NEG}(\text{ST}[A]) = \text{ST}[\sim A]$$

---

[6] See footnote 4 for explanation of the notation here employed.

and then stipulate

[den 2] $\text{den}_{LE^+}(ST[\sim B],s) = NEG(\text{den}_{LE^+}(ST[B],s))$.

For conjunctions, we require (recall my description-operator is inverted 'I')

[den 3] $\text{den}(ST[B\&C],s) = (IX)(\forall Y)(\text{Cons}(Y,X) \leftrightarrow$
$Y = \text{den}(ST[B],s) \vee$
$Y = \text{den}(ST[C],s))$

and accompany this with a schematic axiomatic provision

[AX CONJ] $ST[B\&C] = (IX)(\forall Y)(\text{Cons}(Y,X) \leftrightarrow$
$Y = ST[B] \vee Y = ST[C])$.

And to cover quantifications we put

[den 4] $\text{den}(ST[(\forall v)B],s) = (IX)(\forall Y)(\text{Cons}(Y,X)$
$\leftrightarrow (\exists s')(s' \text{ differs from } s \text{ at}$
most in its assignment to v &
$Y = \text{den}(ST[B],s')))$

and accompany this too with an axiom schema

[AX QUANT] $ST[(\forall v)B] = (IX)(\forall Y)(\text{Cons}(Y,X)$
$\leftrightarrow (\exists v)(Y = ST[B]))$.

In the context of a surrounding truth-theory constructed in a straightforwardly Tarskian fashion adapted only to provide for the many-sorted nature of the variables of LE^+, these requirements on denotation and their accompanying axiomatic provisions will serve to generate all instances of [IV'], as a simple induction on the complexity of state-terms will establish; and with [IV'] in hand, [IV], [III] and finally [II] follow in turn.

The axiom-schemata [AX CONJ] and [AX QUANT] this procedure appeals to are, it is worth noting, entirely *sound*, in the sense that any instance of them finds an explication which is a thesis of the theory of states of affairs of *MLE*. More dubious at first glance, perhaps, is the appeal made to 'NEG' in the treatment of negation, particularly as it is an excrescence not envisaged when the resources of $[LE^+]^*$ were first adumbrated. But then we could easily have formulated LE^+ itself in such a way as to have it already equipped with this functor, and explicated it in *MLE* in a way which validates its governing axiom [AX

NEG].[7] True, that would supply LE^+ with a new way of generating second-level terms, and accordingly require extension to the stipulations already given assigning denotations to such terms; but the necessary addition is untroublesome, since provided by the straightforwardly Tarskian

[den 5] $\text{den}(\text{NEG}(t),s) = \text{NEG}(\text{den}(t,s))$.

9. LE^+, then, admits of the construction, by an extension of Tarskian methods, of an austerely adequate theory of truth cast in the metalanguage $[LE^+]^*$, and apt for construal as a theory of sense. Accordingly, we may embrace paraphrases of adverbial sentences into LE^+ as our final candidates for the base paraphrases of mode adverbial English sentences which Chapter One sought, and note that for good measure our investigation has yielded as well candidates for base paraphrases of causal English sentences, again in the shape of their renditions into LE^+. The base paraphrases of adverbial sentences which we have ended up advocating bear a striking similarity to those Davidson proposed – unsurprisingly, since our key idea has been to develop his basic insight that mode adverbs are best construed as event-predicates. The difference is that this time the base paraphrases advocated are cast within the framework of an explication of key concepts employed within the set-theoretic metalanguage *MLE*, thus providing the explanatory theoretical underpinning which, Chapter One argued, Davidson's own proposals lacked. The fact that our investigation has thus happily yielded an answer to the problems Chapter One set will of course be less impressive to those who take issue with the conception of semantics Chapter One enshrines. But the discussion has been forced along the way to range sufficiently widely for me to hope nevertheless that even such readers will find the work to have at least the mixed merits of the curate's egg.

[7] Just extend the explication ex of the Postscript with the requirement that $[\text{NEG}(t)]^{ex}$ is $<\sim,t^{ex}>$.

Postscript to Chapter 5

To get precise about the way LE^+ sentences find their explications in MLE, define the explication $[A]^{ex}$ of a wff A of LE^+ recursively by the following provisions:

(i) If A is a first-level wff, and t a first-level term, of LE^+, then $[A]^{ex}$ is A and $[t]^{ex}$ is t;

(ii) $[V_i]^{ex}$ is ξ_i, where V_i is LE^+'s i-th state variable and ξ_i is MLE's i-th variable over elements of Σ_{LE};

(iii) $[ST[A]]^{ex}$ is $<\text{Int}_{LE}(P^n), t_1 \ldots t_n>$, when

$A = P^n t_1 \ldots t_n$ for some first-level P^n

and $t_1 \ldots t_n$;

is $<\sim, [B]^{ex}>$ when $A = \sim B$ for some B;

is $\{[B]^{ex}, [C]^{ex}\}$ when

$A = (B\&C)$ for some B and C;

is $\{\xi | (\exists v_i) (\xi = [B]^{ex})\}$ when $A = (\forall v_i)$ B

for some v_i and B;

(iv) $[Ev(t)]^{ex}$ is $(\exists \eta^*)(\eta^* = [t]^{ex})$; $[Con(t,t')]^{ex}$ is

$(\exists \xi)(\xi = [t']^{ex}$ & $[t]^{ex} \in \xi)$; $[Ob(t)]^{ex}$ is $[t]^{ex}$ obtains$_{LE}$;

$[t = t']^{ex}$ is $[t]^{ex} = [t']^{ex}$;

(v) $[VIOLENT(t)]^{ex}$ is $(\exists \eta *)(\eta * = [t]^{ex} \ \& \ Violent(\eta *))$;

     $[WITH(t,t')]^{ex}$ is $(\exists \eta *)(\eta * = [t]^{ex} \ \& \ With(\eta *, [t']^{ex}))$; . . .

(vi)   If A is a complex wff of second level, then:

     $[A]^{ex}$ is $\sim[B]^{ex}$ when A is $\sim$B for some B;

       is $([B]^{ex} \ \& \ [C]^{ex})$ when A is (B&C) for some

       B and C;

       is $(\forall \xi_i) \ [B]^{ex}$ or $(\forall v_i) \ [B]^{ex}$ when A is

       $(\forall V_i)B$ or $(\forall v_i)B$.

Then the LE^+ paraphrases (1iii), (19aiii) and (19biii) are explicated by the *MLE* versions (1ii), (19aii), (19bii) under ex, in the sense that applying ex to the definitional expansions of the LE^+ formulae yields a formula equivalent in *MLE* to the *MLE* paraphrases given.

Bibliography

Anscombe, G.E.M., 'Causality and Extensionality', *Journal of Philosophy* LXVI (1969) pp. 152–159.

Austin, J.L., 'A Plea for Excuses', in his *Philosophical Papers* (second edition; Oxford University Press, 1970), pp. 175–204.

Austin, J.L., *How to Do Things with Words* (Oxford University Press, 1962).

Burge, Tyler, 'Demonstrative Constructions, Reference, and Truth', *Journal of Philosophy* LXXI (1974), pp. 205–223.

Chomsky, Noam, *Aspects of the Theory of Syntax* (M.I.T. Press, 1965).

Clark, Romane, 'Concerning the Logic of Predicate Modifiers', *Noûs* 4 (1970), pp. 311–335.

Davidson, Donald, 'Causal Relations', *The Journal of Philosophy* LXIV (1967), pp. 691–703.

Davidson, Donald, 'Reply to Martin', in Joseph Margolis (ed.) *Fact and Existence* (Blackwell, 1969), pp. 74–83.

Davidson, Donald, 'Semantics for Natural Languages', in Bruno Visentini *et al* (edd.) *Linguaggi nella societa e nella tecnica* (Edizioni di Communita, 1970), pp. 177–188.

Davidson, Donald, 'The Individuation of Events', in Nicholas Rescher *et al* (ed.) *Essays in Honour of Carl G. Hempel* (Reidel, 1969), pp. 216–234.

Davidson, Donald, 'The Logical Form of Action Sentences', in Nicholas Rescher (ed.) *The Logic of Decision and Action* (Pittsburgh University Press, 1974), pp.188–221.

Davidson, Donald, 'Truth and Meaning', *Synthese* 17 (1967), pp. 304–323.

Davidson, Donald, 'True to the Facts', *Journal of Philosophy* LXVI (1969), pp. 748–764.

Davies, Martin, *Meaning, Quantification, Necessity: Themes in Philosophical Logic* (Routledge and Kegan Paul, 1981).

Dowty, David, 'Toward a Semantic Analysis of Verb Aspect and the English "Imperfective" Progressive', *Linguistics and Philosophy* 1 (1977), pp. 45–78.

Dowty, David, *Word Meaning and Montague Grammar* (Reidel, 1979).

Dummett, Michael, 'What is a Theory of Meaning? [II]', in Gareth Evans and John McDowell (edd.) *Truth and Meaning* (Oxford University Press, 1976), pp. 67–137.

Goldman, Alvin, *A Theory of Human Action* (Prentice-Hall, 1970).

Grandy, Richard, 'A Definition of Truth for Theories with Intensional Definite Description Operators', *Journal of Philosophical Logic* 1 (1972), pp. 137–155.

Hornsby, Jennifer, *Actions* (Routledge and Kegan Paul, 1980).

Hornsby, Jennifer, 'Verbs and Events', in Jonathan Dancey (ed.) *Papers on Logic and Language* (Keele University Library, 1980), pp. 88–111.

Kim, Jaegwon, 'Events as Property-Exemplifications', in Myles Brand and Douglas Walton (edd.) *Action Theory* (Reidel, 1976), pp. 159–178.

Kim, Jaegwon, 'On the Psycho-Physical Identity Theory', *American Philosophical Quarterly* 3 (1966), pp. 227–235.

Lewis, David, *Counterfactuals* (Blackwell, 1973).

Martin, R.M., 'On Events and Event-Descriptions', in Joseph Margolis (ed.) *Fact and Existence* (Blackwell, 1969), pp. 63–73.

McDowell, John, 'On the Sense and Reference of a Proper Name', *Mind* 86 (1977), pp. 159–185.

McDowell, John, 'Truth Conditions, Bivalence and Verificationism', in Gareth Evans and John McDowell (edd.) *Truth and Meaning* (Oxford University Press, 1976), pp. 42–66.

McKinsey, J.C.C., 'A New Definition of Truth', *Synthese* 7 (1948/9), pp. 428–433.

Montague, Richard, 'English as a Formal Language', in his *Formal Philosophy* (Yale University Press, 1974), pp. 188–221.

Morton, Adam, 'Extensional and Non-Truth-Functional Contexts', *Journal of Philosophy* LXVI (1969), pp. 159–164.

Parsons, Terence, 'Review of Dowty's *Word Meaning and Montague Grammar*', *The Philosophical Review* 91 (1982), pp. 290–295.

Reichenbach, Hans, *Elements of Symbolic Logic* (Macmillan, 1947).

Russell, Bertrand, 'The Philosophy of Logical Atomism', in David Pears (ed.) *Russell's Logical Atomism* (Fontana, 1972), pp. 31–142.

Scott, Dana, 'Existence and Description in Formal Logic', in Ralph Schoenman (ed.) *Bertrand Russell: Philosopher of the Century* (Allen and Unwin, 1967), pp. 181–200.

Searle, J.R. *Speech Acts* (Cambridge University Press, 1969).

Stalnaker, Robert. See under Thomason.

Strawson, P.F., 'On Referring', *Mind* 59 (1950), pp. 320–344.

Tarski, A., 'The Concept of Truth in Formalized Languages', in his *Logic, Semantics, Metamathematics* (Oxford University Press, 1956), pp. 152–278.

Taylor, Barry, 'States of Affairs', in Gareth Evans and John McDowell (edd.) *Truth and Meaning* (Oxford University Press, 1976), pp. 263–284.

Taylor, Barry, 'Tense and Continuity', *Linguistics and Philosophy* 1 (1977), pp. 199–220.

Taylor, Barry, 'Truth Theory for Indexical Languages', in Mark Platts (ed.)

Reference, Truth and Reality (Routledge and Kegan Paul, 1980), pp. 182–198.

Thomason, Richmond & Stalnaker, Robert, 'A Semantic Theory of Adverbs' *Linguistic Inquiry* 4 (1973), pp. 195–220.

Van Fraassen, Bas, 'Facts and Tautological Entailments', *Journal of Philosophy* 66 (1969), pp. 477–487.

Vlach, Frank, 'The Semantics of the Progressive', in P. Tedeschi and R. Lakoff (edd.) *Syntax and Semantics Volume 14: Tense and Aspect* (Academic Press, 1981), pp. 271–292.

Weinstein, Scott, 'Truth and Demonstratives', *Noûs* 8 (1974), pp. 179–184.

Wiggins, David, 'Verbs and Adverbs, and Some Other Modes of Grammatical Combination', forthcoming from Oxford University Press in a *Festschrift* for Donald Davidson edited by Merrill Provence Hintikka and Bruce Vermazen.

Wilson, N.L., 'Facts, Events and their Identity-Conditions', *Philosophical Studies* 25 (1974), pp. 303–321.

Wittgenstein, Ludwig, *Tractatus Logico-Philosophicus* translated by D.F. Pears and B.F. McGuiness (Routledge and Kegan Paul, 1961).

Index